C000186113

Time to Wake Up
Your life is calling

Irene Remelie

Time to Wake Up...
Your life is calling

First published in 2018

Copyright © Irene Remelie 2018

ISBN: 978-1-9995894-0-0

TEAMAUTHOR UK
Publishing with you

DEDICATION

This book is dedicated to my amazing mum and dad, my
four brothers and sister, all my family and close friends
who have always showed me both sides to the story of life
and who have all helped me to become who I am today.

My husband and best friend Dan who has been my
constant support, my 2 children Amelie and Noah
who are a blessing.

I give my thanks to EVERY single person whom I have
ever known, for you have helped shape me to experience
life in every way.

I dedicate this book to you: the reader.
For together we are writing the story of life.

"I bring you nothing but angels" is my favourite saying
and everyone I have ever had contact with has been
exactly that. Angels. A chance for me to know who I am.
To grow and learn from you all in this
magical experience called life.

Introduction

Hello and a warm welcome to you if this book has come into your hands.

It has come for a reason. YOU, believe it or not, have been looking for some answers, looking for a change, you have been soul searching and this book has appeared to you because you have called it into your life. I know this because as you will discover later on in my book, nothing happens by accident. In this book from my own experience I aim to offer a platform. A way that you can finally take charge of your life and create all that you have ever wanted.

Is it time for you to wake up? Is it time you realised why certain things were happening in your life?

Have you ever questioned why the same thing always seems to happen to you? Are you fed up with not getting anywhere and wondering why?

Do you feel like the world has handed you a raw deal? And that you can't control anything?

Do you feel part of a rat race, forever going in circles and not getting anywhere?

Are you happy with your lot in life? Frustrated with trying to get somewhere but never quite reaching your goals? Struggle with relationships? Low self-esteem? Wondering why you just never seem to get it right? Fed up with the way people treat you?

Are you sick and tired of being sick and tired?

If you are, you may not want to hear this but it is TIME TO WAKE UP!

You have complete control to change it all right now no matter how bad your situation is.

YOUR FUTURE is in your hands and it's very precious indeed so make the most of your time here and have everything you ever wanted. It is not a matter of being LUCKY or knowing the right people, it's all about YOU and once you get YOU right, everything else will fall into place.

I want to reassure you that by no means has my life been a walk in the park and I have had struggles just like you, I could tell you stories of my life that would have you in floods right now BUT that's not what I am here for. I am here to share with you our god given right to be happy and have all we want from life, be it more love, more friends, financial freedom, peace of mind when we choose to WAKE UP!

I once felt like many of the above, in fact I was constantly frustrated and always seeking to find pure happiness, completeness. However, no matter what I did I still felt empty and frustrated. Like everyone was getting ahead in life except me. Until finally I nearly died to get the answers.

The reality is you don't need to have a near death experience to wake up. You don't need to put yourself in the positions I did to see a change, you just need to be aware of how you have come to be where you currently are and the miracle that is called 'Life' and how you can create the life you want and most definitely deserve.

I came to realise a long time ago that I had been what I call sleep walking through most of my life.

In fact, I realised that most people were. I could see people living day in, day out but they were not really living more just existing. What became clear to me was that most people didn't even know they were doing it!

They were so caught up in their minds and none stop thinking that they were not really experiencing life on any level other than automation.

That's when I woke up. However, it came through the most horrific experiences and almost physical death – and personally I would have much rather woke up the easy way.

If you have arrived at this book, then you are clearly ready to wake up and your soul is calling you to remember who you are and why you are here on this planet. Maybe you have already woke up but are being called again to remember.

It is wanting you to become aware of what is happening and how you too have become a slave to your mind and living a life you clearly did not desire for yourself.

This could be the most powerful information you could have brought yourself to know.

My Life in a Nutshell

I have had the jobs I always wanted in TV and radio, hosted events to thousands of people, won cars and holidays, travelled the world and now am a stay at home mum with my partner Dan and 2 beautiful children, Amelie and Noah whilst running a business which allows me to have complete freedom. Now don't get me wrong, this is real life and of course I still encounter problems just like everyone else BUT I have learnt to deal with them differently. Life certainly was not this way for a very long time. It was only when I woke up that I was able to create the life I now have.

Never in life have I been one of these people who just plod on through life, in fact sometimes I wish I could have been, but that was not to be the case for me.... my childhood memories are very vague however I was very blessed to have a big family: 4 brothers and 1 sister who all helped my mum and dad take care of me – my parents worked hard and even when times were hard they always put food on the table (even if it was just a bowl of beans). The most important thing I remember about my childhood was that I was never alone and I feel blessed to have had such a big family – I was very curious about life and would always ask questions – that was something that would stay with me for life. From my teenage years, I became very curious about the supernatural and looked into everything I could get my hands on. I studied physics, witches, ghosts, God and the list went on. In fact throughout my teenage life, I was to experience lots of paranormal and poltergeist activity, a lot I now believe to be partly due to hormones, raising my vibration and becoming more aware of life on this planet. After these experiences, I was always looking for the answers. I also had some very strange experiences myself which woke me up to the fact there was much more to life than I was aware of.

I went to school and had many of the experiences we all have, bullying and all the emotions that come with growing up.

I was very lucky to have a big family. My family was rich in life because we had love and support however financially we lived a normal life and went through struggles like most people – this I feel was my starting point as I decided at a very young age that I wanted to do everything I possibly could.

From the age of 10, I worked on my brother's milk round before school so I could fund myself to go to a private dance school. I was always wanting to express myself and dance; acting and singing seemed to be the way forward. I worked throughout my school education doing the milk round and also got myself a weekend job working at a golf course.

I didn't come out of school with the best grades but enough to take me into drama school.

Once I finished drama school and also after a relationship that broke my heart, I packed my bags and went off to travel the world. I bungee-jumped in rain forests, swam with dolphins, and did any job possible that would fund my trip from cleaning toilets to silver service waitressing. I did most jobs that I wanted to do and life was good — I was very blessed to be a very positive person (most of the time). Even though life was good, there were still questions about life that were in the background of my mind — I would often ask myself questions like: what's the point in life, why am I here? Something felt like it was missing and I could not quite put my finger on it. I went on to delve more into the world of physics, mystics, ghosts and attended many spiritual churches in search for my answers only to still not find what I was looking for — but I knew I was getting close.

Over the following years, I worked different jobs, and also continued acting and singing in my spare time. I put myself in various abusive relationships and just plodded through life living one day to the next.

I was always trying to better myself, looking for the next big break, working long hours and basically trying every which way to become a singer or an actor.

Years were spent entering competitions and being rejected by agents. Anywhere I ever got was through hard work.

In this time, I qualified to become a holistic therapist but eventually became involved in the radio as a promotions girl. Handing out stickers and basically interacting with the public.

The real change happened in the year 2007. I was then working in radio in promotions and was also married – which at that time was not going well. I was in a bad place and desperate to sort out my life. I could just not cope with my life situations at that time and needed some drastic changes but did not have a clue where to start. I had run myself ragged working so hard, that I spent a lot of time crying. I felt lost and useless.

It was at that time that I collapsed in my bedroom and prayed. I had no idea what I was doing but I prayed to God to sort out my life (I remember I was crying so much I could barely breathe). What was to follow would be the biggest wake-up call of my life. I really could see no way forward in life and got to the point where I wanted to run away from everything. In a way I often thought I would be better off dead.

What happened after this event in the weeks to come would be the start of my wake-up call. Just weeks later, I was involved in a car accident which resulted in me breaking both my knees, my ribs and various other injuries and being put in intensive care in hospital. I was there for 8 weeks and whilst in intensive care I was heavily dosed on morphine and often believed I was in heaven. I remember at one point my entire family surrounded me in my hospital bed. I could not move and had many drips hanging off me; they were all looking at me like I would not be here much longer and I remember thinking it's taken a car crash to gather all my family in the room at the same time, something that would normally only happen at birthdays and Christmas.

Little did I know that this car crash would turn my life upside down.

Looking back on my life now, it is so clear to me why all the events had led me to this place in time and gave me the understanding to know that EVERYTHING happens for a reason, nothing is by accident and it all serves a purpose.

When I had the car crash, my job was working as an outside radio presenter, which basically meant I was out on the streets mixing with the public doing live links back into a breakfast show. I also would do stunts, play jokes and generally had a lot of fun.

Because my job was mostly driving and I had broken my knees, I could no longer walk let alone drive, so for the next 12 months I was house-bound.

This is when my ultimate journey began or what I should say this is when for the first time in my life I was waking up.

My life so far had been better than average through continual hard slog but I realised I had played part of it rather than have control over it.

For the first time I could understand Shakespeare's quote: 'the world is a stage and we are all actors'. I had been drifting, blissfully unaware of what life was really all about AND although life had been great on many levels there had always been a niggling at the back of my mind that there was still something more. I still wanted that peace that I knew in my heart was missing and the car crash was about to give me that.

For the next 12 months I was about to experience all things not normal: out of body experiences, hearing voices, synchronicity would play so strong in my life that before the phone even rang I knew who it was going to be, the lights would switch on and off, kettle turn itself on and tv channel turn itself over and for a while I thought I was going crazy. I really didn't know what was going on and even worse I didn't know who I was. At one point I believed I was clearly going crazy and even though it may be down to the pain killers I was on, soon I was to know that this was all part of my wake-up call.

In that 12 months I must have read close to 40 books.

This process continued for the next few years where all manner of strange things would happen. I would think of something, then the following day it would turn up in my life. I would walk in a book shop and a book would fall off the shelf at me.

I felt like I was in a film, that someone was trying to tell me something. None of these things would scare me anymore; they were becoming part of my daily life. If I had a question in my head the following phone call, reading a paper, listening to a song would have the answer for me. For this reason, I knew I was not going crazy as the answer was always provided. At this time I also went through a divorce and ended up living on my own for the first time ever...throughout all of these challenges, although heart-breaking and emotional, I was very much living in a whirlwind. A couple of years went by getting to grips with all that happened and also coming to understand why they had happened.

After that I went on to get my dream job: have my own breakfast show and I got a tv show. I won a car on The Price is Right, won holidays and the list of amazing things just went on. Life just became absolutely amazing. Miracles seemed to happen before my eyes. I had harnessed all of my experiences and realised that I was in fact in control of what was now happening to me, and that I had been all along.

I came to realise that most of the experiences in my adulthood, I had created. I had been playing victim to my situations rather than seeing that I always had had choices, even if they didn't seem to be ones that I wanted.

I don't want this book to turn into a story about my life but to just give you a brief idea about who I was and how, should you wish to turn your life around as well, you can.

This book is aimed to open your mind to a new way of thinking and to offer tools for you to change your own life and start turning things round in favour for you but to do this first of all we have to look at some things to open your mind up to all the possibilities that lie ahead for you. For once you understand who you really are then all things are made possible.

For the next few chapters we are going to take you out of your comfort zone. We are going to talk about things that may not normally come up in your daily conversations. We need to do this so that you can question all this for yourself. To choose what is real for you and to find out for yourself what you really want from life. I would like to point out that this is what I have come to find out to be MY truth. The aim throughout this book is to encourage you to find your truth.

I would also like to say that this is a very different way of life for some people reading this for the first time. You may feel some of it's too good to be true and if that is the case, then ask yourself the question, *if at the very least it makes me feel more positive, then what do I have to lose?*

What I am about to go through in this book may be nothing new for you, for you already have all the answers you need inside. You have brought yourself to this book to remember who you are. Therefore, what I share here is nothing ground-breaking or anything that has not been covered throughout the ages, but hopefully enough to open your eyes to your own life.

It is you calling yourself to be reminded of your purpose. In fact on many occasions when you read this you will recognise that you already know, however you are merely sleep-walking and are about to wake-up and remember who you are!

Where the World is Now

"The world is forever changing, some changes appear bad and others appear good, either way, you will see in the world what you give your focus to."

It is a very challenging world that we live in now and to be honest many would say the state of our planet, the horrendous things that happen would lead you to believe that it's not a great time to be here. All the positive quotes in the world couldn't plaster over the world we live in. In fact it's blooming heart-breaking to even try and comprehend how these things could be happening in such an evolved world which is so advanced in many ways, yet can be so destructive at the same time. It's almost soul-destroying watching the human race treat each other the way that it does. It's like an endless conveyer belt of destruction and death when we all know that there is more than enough for everyone.

You yourself may often ask the question, "how can this be happening?" Watching the news on a daily basis is enough to make anyone cry. This is where the term 'sleep walking' comes into play. Most people are living on automation and have become so desensitized from who they really are that they feel they have no control over anything, even what's happening to them on an individual level.

We are at a time where people have had enough and are constantly asking questions. Many think this is a bad thing when in fact this is just the beginning. People are asking the questions which will in turn help them to wake up. The main problem is that people just don't know how they can impact on their own lives or the world that surrounds them.

Many people are trying through positive thinking, being healthy, joining a cause and the list goes on that people are grasping at straws for some clarity about how this could possibly happen and what can we do to change it. People are in power who seem to have control. Everywhere we look there are challenges, even across social media platforms there is doom and gloom leading us to believe we have less choices and no control.

There are many people who are trying to combat that with many techniques using positive aspects to life on this planet. These are all fantastic ways to help. Many self-help books, courses, mindfulness, mediation and a wide variety of platforms provide information that is easy to access. The good news is, there is more good in this world than bad.

The great news is that you can have a bigger impact on it all.

If you're reading this then you may have already come across the law of attraction and tried to implement that into your own life. This is the process of where thoughts become things. Many have tried this positive thinking without much success and questioned if it really works. For me, I believe that is because they have missed the key ingredient in this process, which we will talk more about later.

The good news is people are waking up, they are questioning life, their purpose, why they are here, how they can make life better.

Many feel that life is just hard slog, feeling they work harder and harder and get nowhere. That the rich get richer and it doesn't matter what effort they do or how much harder they work, it just never seems to get easier.

Society has created many divides between people, creating an 'us' and 'them' when the truth is, we are all in the same boat, just some have oars and some don't.

Although there are many challenges on a global scale right now and we feel out of control, I believe this will change as more and more people come to question this and in turn start to wake up. They will in fact, take control of their own lives which in turn will massively impact the world in which we live.

When you start to ask the bigger questions in life, like: Who am I? Why am I here? What is my purpose? And you get to understand what your truth is for you, then life takes on a whole new meaning.

Who Am I? Who Are You?

This has to be one of the biggest questions of life. Who are we? Where did we come from? Life after death? Is there a God?

There are a couple of things to consider in this area and also what sits right with you. After all, this book is about helping you to find your truth and in understanding who we are it's a great starting point for you to come to terms with the fact that whatever your belief system, you are a miracle.

We have many points of reference, the bible versus science and many different religions and no matter where you sit with this, here is something to bear in mind regardless of what side of the fence you sit on.

Firstly, words are just labels. God, Buddha, universal energy, science...etc. They are a name we give to something to explain it. Everything that has happened in life has had to have been put into words to explain it to people and words can be interpreted in many ways.

Let's take science for a moment. How could science possibly tie in with God? After all, so many people believe in the big bang. My purpose is not to point you in one direction or the other but just to show you some of the links and possibilities you may be able to perceive about the bigger picture of life.

Out of my experiences I came to study quantum physics and without going technical and confusing, what it points to is the fact that everything is made up of energy. Every single thing on this planet: you, me, a car, a tree, a table and anything and everything.

We are all energy just vibrating at different frequencies. Energy is all around us. Wind is one of the most powerful energy sources; it can cause chaos, blow down trees, destroy houses and all sorts yet we cannot physically see it, only the effects of it! The same as a phone. You can speak over a piece of plastic to someone in a different country which is all powered by energy and vibrations. Yet to the physical eye it cannot be seen.

You only need to look at all the amazing things around you such as your tv, kettle, street lights; all are powered by invisible energy to the naked eye. It is fact that our body is made up of energy also.

So, what about your thoughts? You can't see them or touch them but they too are made of energy. So, if you can imagine your thoughts are just like the wind, you can't see them but they are affecting everything in your life and attracting it to you.

We were talking about words just being things to represent something. Some people may call energy God, universal energy, science and other names. Either way it boils down to the same thing that can be explained scientifically as fact. An energy source.

Therefore, ultimately we are all connected on some level and what frequency we put out we will attract back to us; a bit like when you're trying to find your favourite radio station you have to keep going till you get the right connection.

So, if we are all connected and all the same, then maybe consider the idea that what you hold in your head you will attract more of. If you're sending out bad vibes you will match a similar bad vibe frequency.

For the purpose of this book, I am going to call energy 'God'. All that is, the omega, beginning and end.

I don't personally see God as a male figure with a white beard as I did when I was a child. I see God as the energy of love.

Here lies the big question, if there is a God then why do so many bad things happen in life?

We have free will, we choose what to fill our heads and lives with. Scientifically, energy cannot be destroyed therefore it will never end.

Where does the wind begin and end? Where does the sky begin and end? If energy cannot be destroyed, then it must vibrate at a different frequency or change form.

The problems we encounter here on this planet are what we have created ourselves as a society and individually through our thinking and feeling.

We are creating our world and that's where we need to take responsibility for the role we choose to play in it and where we focus our time and energy.

Only when we choose to wake up will we change our own lives and the lives of others. For taking responsibility for ourselves, affects not only our lives but everyone around us.

When the question is asked, who are we? The answer is never simple, but if you look at it as we are part of the all that is and ever will be, you are a unique soul in a body, having an experience on this planet. In the same way we have a car as a vehicle, we as energy, a soul, a part of God, have come here to have an experience and as energy is invisible to the physical eye, we would need a physical form to enjoy the physical experience.

I want to suggest an idea to you that may or may not fit into your belief system and again, this is going to need you be open-minded.

We have much historical facts about why we are here and where we have come from, but I want to offer this as suggestion to you.

In the beginning there was an energy; let's call that energy love/God. That was all there was. That love was an energy source and because there was nothing else, it actually didn't know what it was (to know what something is, you have to have the opposite). To know what light is, you would need to know darkness, to know what 'up' is you would need to know what 'down' was. To know 'hot' you need to know 'cold'. However, there was just this gigantic energy and nothing else.

Many believe in the big bang theory so let's go with that for the purpose of this explanation.

There came a time when the only way this 'love energy' would know what is was, was by breaking and separating so that it could see itself from a different angle. It needed an opposite to be able to know and experience that was what it is was. In comes the world. With all its wonder...ever-expanding and growing. Plants, animals, humans and a fantastic planet for that energy to experience who it is and can be. Now, whether you believe in the Big Bang, God creating the world in seven days or science or evolution...we all originate from the same source. A source of love that has come to experience who we are. We are an individual aspect of all that is.

Let's put that in simple terms. There is an ocean, big and vast and never ending. It is one giant ocean however, it has individual waves and ripples. It's never separate, it is still the same but shows up in different ways. Be it a wave, a ripple, a stream, a lake...it's all part of the same source. It is all equal.

We are no different, EVERYTHING is made up from energy therefore we are also part of the bigger picture, part of God, love energy, the source or whatever label you would like to call it.

That's pretty amazing don't you think? That you, right now reading this, are part of all that is and ever will be! You are here in physical form to experience life.

So many would ask the question, 'does that make me God'? And the answer is yes, you are part of God, just like the wave is part of the ocean.

You are a unique expression of God experiencing itself.

The next question then is, if I am part of God then why can't I walk on water and make miracles happen in my life? I say that in jest however, it's a perfectly good question and the answer to this can be found in some of the natural laws of our world. There a few things that are certain and factual like the fact we come into physical body, we are born and we eventually die and leave the body.

There is also a fact of gravity and natural laws in place that are scientifically proven about energy. Like attracts like. Similar to a magnet. We attract to us what we think about most. Be it good or bad. Just like gravity has no preference, nor does energy. It attracts what is focused on.

We were given a mind as a tool to be able to attract what we want into our lives, to use the power of our thoughts to create the experiences we want. However, this is not something we are taught from a young age. Instead we are taught to go into the system that is known as school, educate ourselves then go get a job. No one ever pulled us to one side and said you can create your life by the thoughts you hold so we all got plugged into a system with limiting beliefs and just accepted it as our reality. There is ample information to suggest that many people knew that thoughts became things. That anyone could have anything and those people didn't like the thought of not having power and control and instead of understanding it was limitless and provide no end to greatness, they got greedy and decided to keep that knowledge to themselves which many believe is why systems were put in place to control us, to keep that information from us.

This came in the forms of religious groups, systems and institutions that have been rolled out throughout the world.

In the Bible you will hear phrases from Jesus such as…

'Ask and it is given'.

'You are all capable of this and more'.

Even in the Bible itself we are told that we are God's children with everything at the heart of what Jesus said.

'Love one and another'.

'We are all family'.

Everything he stood for was complete understanding, compassion, being non-judgemental. He told people they could heal themselves and others 'To go out and spread the word of love'.

I am not in any way trying to disrespect anyone's beliefs. I am just trying to open your eyes to who you really are. You are, at your very essence, love.

Why Are We Here?

"The question is not why are we here, it is what do you want to experience whilst you are."

Many people can go through life without even asking that question, and if they are happy, then that's wonderful, however for many, happiness is something they feel they have to attain.

Have you ever asked yourself: why I am here? Do you even care why you are here? Well, if you do, then that is a great place to start.

In the grander scheme of life many will say: what's the purpose of life? Some believe they are sent here for tests, some believe we are here through evolution, some believe in religion, others believe in nothing – either way, whatever you believe in, have you ever asked the question of the miracles around you? How amazing that life truly is and what we have created on this planet? I don't believe anyone in this life can give a factual 'one right answer' as we are evolving constantly. What we can say though, is that NO ONE

KNOWS ALL THE ANSWERS but that LIFE IN ITSELF IS IN FACT A MIRACLE.

Did you read that? Life is a miracle! YOU are in fact a miracle, a wondrous human being on this planet experiencing life. So, let's just look more deeply at that statement. Let's call this life/energy GOD, an energy force that vibrates through everything and everyone. In fact, if we are all made up of that same energy, does that not in turn make us part of God? The Universe? And in the same breath, does that not make us all connected in some way? If we are all made of the same stuff then surely that means we are all part of the same plan, and if we are all the same stuff then that would mean that actually you and I are the same? That we have come to this planet to experience who we are and all the different feelings, emotions and relationships.

Now, based on what we spoke about in the first chapter and knowing that thoughts and feelings create things and situations, we have done that because we wanted to experience who we are and the only way we can do that is by having experiences that we do or don't like.

As I said earlier, the purpose of separation was so we could know and experience fully the extent of who we are. And we can only really do that by knowing the opposite of who we are not, or don't want to be. What we do and don't want. We learn in life by trying new things to gauge if it's for us or not for us.

For example, you may try a new food. You either like it or don't. If you don't like it, then you don't eat it again but try something different. With experiences we have, it gives us the chance to know if were heading in the direction of sadness or peace. Love or hate.

For example, I look at life like a holiday…one holiday I may want to sit on the beach, another I may want to go on an adventure, do white water rapids, jump out of a plane…but I wouldn't know what I wanted unless I had the opposite of it show up. If I went on holiday and didn't like it, I wouldn't go again but go somewhere different.

Our experiences in life can be looked at in a similar way…If you didn't know heartbreak, you would not know love, if you didn't have pain you would not know joy, if you didn't have happiness you wouldn't know sadness. All experiences help us to know what we do and don't want – they are all contrasts and in turn help us to expand to being a better version of ourselves. So, when the things we deem as horrible show up in our lives it's an opportunity for us to recognise who we want to become next, what we want to experience next.

If the law of attraction is that we bring about what we think about, then is it fair to look at your life right now, think about what you normally think about and see if your life mirrors that? Are you worried about money? Are you worried about work? Are they the main issues in your life right now? Are you focusing on them too much in a negative way?

Do the same and look at the good things in your life. What thoughts do you hold about them? I bet you will be able to see the things you worry about most are constant, whereas the things you give not much energy to are fine.

So…the answer to *why are we here*? If we are here for the experience then I ask you the question, *why* do you want to be here? And, if we are all the same then what is our purpose other than to experience life and attract into it what we want and don't want?

Here is another idea. Let's just say for one moment we are all made up of the same stuff…we are all part of life/God/the Universe…then that would make us all one with each other on some level. This may take a little to open your mind – but let's just say that was the case – that you and I are in fact the same, connected – then that would mean that we are using each other to experience ourselves. Yes, I know that seems very confusing but if we are all one and the same then that would mean we are one and I am writing to myself right now – so what would be the purpose, right? Let's just say that it would be pretty boring on my own here therefore I choose to have the experience of having connections with others and for that reason means I am on this planet to experience life, to experience separation and unity. We have to have an opposite to know what it is. If we are here on this planet to experience life, then ask yourself the question: *what would you like to experience? What would be great for you to do/be/have/give?*

And if we are here purely for experiences and that when we die a physical death that it's not the end, that we return to source to plan our next big holiday of experiences, then would it be fair to say that each time you come down that you may choose something different? An experience of forgiveness, love, loss, hate, or any other form of emotion?

This can be incredibly challenging as that leaves the court wide open for many people to do horrible things but in our journey, it is always happiness, joy, love that we come for. That's what we originate from and we know that's when we're at our most peaceful.

This can be hard to swallow; it was for me especially looking at the world and the way it is, with all the horror that goes on but again, most of that has come from a corrupt way of thinking. From being plugged into a system that never taught us the power we have. We are led to believe in power, greed, money, fighting against the system, fighting against each other. We are led to believe we live in a word of 'lack' which is ludicrous, considering we are making it all up. We print money, grow food yet there is a lack? To our resources? There is none what so other than what man has created.

Ask yourself the question: if people knew that they are what they thought, that they could literally create a life of love, freedom and everything they wanted, do you really think people would choose the opposite?

Unfortunately, things that were put in place to keep us from this knowledge have spread across time and been indoctrinated into our lives. We have known no different.

If we have the power to think better ways, feel better emotions to create the life we want then this is where life gets really exciting; it means you get to choose what you want next.

What do you want to experience? If I were to say to you that you could be/have/do whatever you wanted...would you say that was impossible or would you know deep in your heart that really you are capable of so much and more? Right now, ask yourself what you want, what do you wish to spend your valuable time on this planet doing and then do it! There is nothing stopping you, not even money, nothing. The only thing that will stop you is you.

Did You Put Yourself in a Hole?

"If there's an 'up', there is a 'down', an 'in' then there's an 'out'. If there's a shovel to dig a hole, you can use it to fill it and get back out of it."

By a hole I mean, do you feel you just can't get out of your situation or repetitive cycle?

There are many reasons you may be in a hole; it may be that you're struggling to survive, you may have a high-powered job but are on the brink of a breakdown. You may have done everything you thought possible to make you happy and are still not quite feeling it.

One of the main problems I see people facing right now is that they are ALWAYS waiting for the right time, perfect moment, another day, another week, and next year. Most people are waiting for the next best thing, the big house, the lottery win, the job promotion, the perfect relationship and the list is endless.

I want you to think about this for a second. This could potentially blow your mind.

More often than not, one of the main reasons people want ANYTHING in life is because they believe the 'having' of it will make them feel better. There are a few people that want these things for the sake of it. Ultimately, they want them because they believe they will feel better, life will be better.

When I go on holiday, when I get the promotion, when I find the perfect partner, when I win the lottery, when I GET THIS AND THAT... it's because you believe that having achieved 'that' will make you feel better or even other people around you feel better. So, people live on automation, living each day, longing for the next.

The problem with this is then you're not 'living', you are just existing, and every day seems a struggle often with no joy or happiness in sight. You convince yourself that it's ok to feel that way because you believe you feel that way for the lack of what you don't have.

Let's take this a bit further...if happiness was brought about by the achievement of these things then is it safe to say that every rich person was happy? Because the reality is, many of them are not. You only need to watch the tv or read the newspaper to see many celebrities spiral down, commit suicide, end up in rehab and still encounter the daily problems we all do. You hear stories of lottery winners who lose all their money or become unhappy because their life is no better.

We are all led to believe that money is the solution to our problems and when we don't have any, it becomes easy to allow yourself to feel like crap. That it's understandable because if you just had more money, then life would be perfect. Yes, money can help in many ways, but it is not the answer to your problems. Lack of money is not the reason you are feeling unhappy, unfulfilled and always waiting for the next big thing to bring you some joy for a short period of time.

Joy is at your disposal every second of every day. Therefore, it is key to start becoming aware of how you feel. If something makes you feel good, then that's a great place to start knowing what you really want. For what you *feel* and *think* is what will become your reality, your experience. It is important to feel better, which leads to thinking better and guess what? All of those feel-good things will start to show up in your life.

It's the law! What you give out will come back to you.

You're Not Who You Think You Are

"You are not your past, you are who you decide you want to be, you can create a new you every day."

Who you are right now is not who you think you are (unless you think you're blooming awesome at the core of everything you do...which you are, by the way!)

We get born into the world and into the circumstances and situations we find ourselves, which is out of our control. We may have been blessed to come into the perfect family however, this is very rarely the case because we are all experiencing life so no matter what your childhood was you were bound to face hardships and challenges along the way. We have imprinted on us the people who bring us up, our neighbours, our friends, teachers and every person we come into contact with and at a young age, we take all of that as fact. We accept what we are told and what we are shown. It's only as we become older that we start to become individuals and start making our own choices and decisions.

Although we do that, there is a lot of hard-wiring gone into our minds from an early age. In research it actually states that most of our beliefs, behaviours come from the age of 0 to age 7.

The mind is a tool we are given to store that information. What I come to find is that instead of using it as a tool, that many (including myself) were being used by it.

Our mind is very much like a search engine on your computer. We as humans for many years have been programming our minds with everything that happens around us. Our childhood, our teachers, the tv, the newspapers, everybody else's views and opinions which we took as our own.

In fact, most people believe the experiences we have put on us in younger years are what make us who we are and although partly that's true, it doesn't mean that those experiences are us now in the present.

We're very similar to that search engine. The moment we think of something, see something, hear something our mind searches through all past experiences and brings it to our awareness. We then act out previous/similar scenarios, more often than not unconsciously, because we're running on a programme, using anything from the past to help in that situation.

Now here lies the problem. Sometimes that benefits us and protects us from being harmed but often it has no relevance to our current emotional situation and is why many people keep repeating the same behaviours and patterns through life.

They are not reacting to the present moment BUT living on automation, sleep walking.

This is a challenge for everyone as bear in mind, everything you currently are is made up from every positive and negative experience you have ever had.

There are certain laws in this world and we can get some evidence from quantum physics. Just as gravity states you can chuck a rock out of the window and it will hit the ground, the same can be said for us. We as humans are made up from energy; science states everything around us is made up of energy and vibrates at a different frequency. So, if we're all made up of the same stuff, does that not in fact state that in some way unseen, we're are all connected? Like the vast sea which is one, still we are all individual waves?

So, if we are all energy vibrating at different frequencies and science suggests as a law what we emit comes back to us, is it then fair to say what we think is incredibly powerful?

Science tells us that there is a law of attraction. What you focus on is what you will attract, so our job is to find the frequency we want. We need to spend more time thinking about the big things we DO want rather than the lack of what we DON'T.

The same way you have to find your favourite radio channel by tuning in, we have to tune in to what we want and that can only be done by taking control of your mind and what you put into it. By waking up and taking back the power of your mind.

What I want to do is give you 3 top tips to help you to become more awake.

Tip 1
Feed your mind and create new habits

Read more books. You have had a life of wiring your mind into certain thinking patterns. Many that do not benefit you and some of them not by choice but given to you by those around you. Part of the process is to start changing those programmes and putting new data in so that when you search, you bring new ideas in your mind, with new results. You will have found there will be new answers in there as well, to give you better results in life.

That can be done by creating new habits – once you think or do something over a period of time it becomes a habit, just something you automatically do. That's why when you drive to work you can get there on automation. Your unconscious mind is working for you while your conscious mind can be away with the fairies. Sometimes you get to your job, shop, wherever you're going, and question how you got there because your mind had been on other stuff. Like, did I lock the door? Look at that idiot driver! What shall we eat for tea tonight? And the list goes on.

By feeding your brain with new information and creating new daily habits of thought about what you want from life, you can start to become who you really want to be.

Beliefs create habits. Thinking positively is very different than actually believing.

This, I feel, is where many come unstuck. I know I certainly did. You can say and try to think positive, but if you don't actually FEEL or believe it, then you're just kidding yourself. However, the good news is: a belief is just a thought you keep thinking. That thought then becomes a habit which in turn creates habitual behaviours.

The more you think it, the more you believe it, the more you create it in your life.

The key for change then, is not to try and change that strong belief head on, otherwise you will spend your time arguing with yourself, especially if it's a long-standing belief. Instead, try and nip it gently in the bud when the thought arises. EG... 'I hate my life, I hate everything about it, nothing works out for me, my job is so hard.'

The moment that arises is when you need to try and soften the force by introducing gentler ones and replacing them... 'I can remember a time when I loved my life, I had so much fun, if I have had that once, surely I can have it again?'

'My job seems hard right now, but I recall times when it was very easy and I enjoyed it a lot.'

Create new thought habits and create new behaviour habits.

When you wake in the morning, do you hit the snooze button 10 times and hide under the blanket?

If so, try jumping out of bed as soon as the alarm sounds, have a dance around your kitchen, turn up the music...Instantly you will see how that behaviour transforms your life.

Take a good look at your habits and behaviours now.

Write a list of which feel good and which feel bad then put a plan of action in place to change those that don't benefit you.

TIP 2
Create yourself

You are not your past – you are who you decide to be right now.

If you self-condemn, beat yourself up about who you are and what you did or didn't do, you're just bringing it into your energy and current situation. You are creating more of it and sabotaging yourself.

Decide right now on who you want to be, how you want to show up in the world. What are your boundaries?

What is acceptable to you? How do you want to be treated? What sort of people do you want to be around and associate with? Don't settle for anything less than the new standards you put in place for yourself. Now be that person.

Treat people the way you want to be treated and more of that will come your way.

TIP 3
LOVE

Cheesy, but true.

Love is the highest vibration. Unconditional love for yourself and those around you puts you in the perfect place to attract and receive great things into your life but also it has a ripple effect on those around you.

It's hard to love unconditionally but it's what can give you peace if you're no longer angry at the world, at yourself and those around you. When you accept yourself and others, when you no longer judge yourself and others, you release anger and frustration from your life.

If you see others as an extended version of yourself, that no one is against you and that they are just a mirror image of your deepest thoughts, be it dark or light, you can then look at them as a friend and not an enemy.

You then realise that the fight is not with others but has always been with yourself and how you judge and perceive.

When you hold anger or hate about someone or something, it only creates more of it and pulls it towards you.

The only person the negative thoughts affect are the people that hold them, so anything other than thoughts of love have no benefit to you.

These 3 steps are just the beginning to help wake you up and help those around you be affected by the new energy that you hold. Start to use your mind as a tool and not let it use you.

You Are the Answer

"Often we are too busy looking for solutions outside of ourselves. We forget that no one knows us better than ourselves. We have all the answers right in front of us, it's just a matter of listening to that inner voice."

We can often spend so much time looking outwards for the answers when the truth is, they are already in you – that's right – you hold all the cards, all the answers. The secret is to quiet your mind so you can actually hear yourself – we all can spend years reading self-help books/going to seminars, looking for answers when they have been with us all along. You have the power to know exactly what is right for you once you define negative mind chatter from what you really want – earlier we talked about your mind being a tool that can sometimes over-take who you are. So, who are you? Well, as we have already talked about, we are all part of the big picture, in fact part of God, so who outside would we need? And in fact, if you are the bigger picture then who better to give you the answer, right?

Now it can be difficult and at first you may feel like you're talking to yourself but now is the time to do exactly that. If you don't feel comfortable with that, then call it God/the Universe and simply ask the question – whatever that may be – then wait for the answer. It may come in many ways to you; you may hear it on the next tv advert, the next radio song, the next person who calls you…many ways the answer may come, it may even just pop into your head, but you will attract the right answer you need. When I first started asking for answers, I could not always get my mind quiet or distinguish what was my mind chatter and what was real. The best way you can know what is real will be the highest answer you get, the one that brings you love and good feeling, not the ones that put you down or make you feel bad. That is more likely to be your mind chatter – if you struggle to get quiet and still, then I would strongly recommend meditation to get in touch with yourself and the higher connection. The best time to do this is in the morning – when you have some quiet time – sit down and take deep breaths – maybe focus on a word, for example the word LOVE and keep repeating it to yourself like a mantra. The reason for this is so that when your mind keeps butting in, you can take the focus away again – don't fight your mind – we want it on side so if it does start chirping away at you, then say 'thank you for that thought but it does not serve my purpose of what I am trying to do right now'. Recognise it is only your programmed mind-set that keeps butting in with its old thought processes and then realise that is not who you are but just old thoughts on auto pilot trying to find an answer.

The mind will just relay old experiences to give you an answer and that is why we often repeat the same circles in life – often you will see people in the same relationships, same money problems, same self-abusive patterns and that is because our minds will always go to what they know best or at least think they know best. Every experience should be a new one. We can often create ongoing problems if we let our past mind experiences/patterns dictate what we should now do. Remember, our mind is a tool therefore it feels it is trying to protect us so will use past resources and outcomes to do just that. That's often why we end up going in circle after circle – the key comes when we can recognise that we are not our past experiences but move on from them to make new choices and decisions about where we want to go next.

If you struggle with meditation, maybe join a class or even buy a relaxing cd to get you in the right mood – once you are relaxed, then ask the question you need an answer to. Often it will come straight away. If not, then expect to see an answer in the next few days. When I first started on my journey, I would often ask God for a sign – and then not be able to recognise it as my mind would always say no, that was too obvious... it was just a coincidence. However, there are no coincidences, all things happen for a reason. It's being able to know what that reason is and you can always find that out by asking if it's coming from a place of love. Anger, hate, jealousy are not of benefit to you other than to experience the opposite of it.

Who Controls Your Happiness?

"If you let outside circumstances affect how you feel, you are giving your power to someone else. Only you can choose what you give your focus to and take your power back."

Seems like a silly question, but do you have control over how you *feel*, OR do you allow others to dictate your happiness today?

Sometimes we can take other people's opinions and thoughts on us, as if they were our own. You may have someone in your life at the moment who is determining who you are and how you feel. You may have someone telling you that you're great OR the opposite…that you're worthless!

How do you value yourself? You see, at some point we all have people who don't agree with who we are or what we're doing and that's ok especially if it's someone who really has your concern at heart. BUT, sometimes people can make judgements or comments that are not of constructive help to you and this is where we really need to stay strong about who we are OR want to be. REMEMBER they are someone else's opinions NOT yours. There is no one that knows your situation better than yourself; they do not live your life 24/7 so their opinions are just that. Their **OPINIONS.**

I have had times in the past, just like you where my actions have been questioned, even to the point where it may have made me question myself. I came to learn very long ago that some people's opinions are valuable and they genuinely care about me and want the best for me, then there are others who know nothing about my life OR situation and just think they know it all.

I found that I decided not to let anybody make me question myself! Yes, if they had a point I would take it on board BUT I would not take their opinion as my own, after all it was an outside judgement more often than not with no knowledge to my choice, be it my choice to go travelling, change jobs and the list goes on.

A way to help you deal with yourself and others is ask the question. *What would this situation look like if I came at it from love? What would love do next?*

This made life so much more enjoyable, anytime anything happened in my life, I would try to resolve the situation with that question and the answer always seemed clearer. Don't get me wrong, sometimes it was a little difficult, especially if you're having a fall out with your partner, or someone you completely disagree with and you feel like fighting and defending yourself BUT, ultimately attacking someone will only lead to more destruction. By allowing people to have their own opinions and judgements and not make judgements back to them, it allows you to accept others for who they are. By accepting, it doesn't mean you agree, but it means you accept their choices for them.

Coming from the place of LOVE allows you to deal with life to the best of your ability. The old saying, *never judge a book by its cover*, often rings true to me. We often want to help people but sometimes people don't want help.

We'll look at a situation someone is in and think they are crazy! Why are they still in that job or why are they still with that partner? But, we don't know the inside of that book. Sometimes you may actually be right, but if someone does not want to help themselves, who are we to force on them? However, you can help them in a different way: LOVE.

LOVE for me is God, Universe, energy...all that is. It's unconditional, it's accepting, it's forgiveness. You can forgive someone for their dreadful behaviour, it does not mean by forgiving you have to keep allowing them to treat you dreadful. For me it means, I cannot change someone's behaviour, but I can change my behaviour towards them.

Value yourself enough to not let others' opinions become your own about yourself and don't let someone take your happiness away. We can't control how others behave but, we can control how we let it affect our joy!

Is Being Happy a Choice?

Now many of you will say: NO NO NO, IT'S NOT! but through my experience I have found that for me, it certainly is.

We ALL encounter problems, every single one of us is human so for that reason alone we face difficulties every day. For some, it can be life threatening and for others it may seem small, like my phone won't work, but you can be sure we are all in the same boat and at some point in our lives will encounter similar situations, be it family, friends, partners, work, money, health, death, and so on.

After speaking with a close friend who has experienced cancer on 2 occasions but is still extremely positive, it was a lovely reminder to me how she had chosen to deal with it in a positive way rather than sink into depression. After all, nearly losing your life on 2 occasions and dealing with treatments, financial worries and family heartache, it's going to take its toll on you. Surprisingly, because of the way she dealt with it, it had a knock-on effect on her friends and family.

Because she was strong, they were; because she held it together, they did. Yes, sometimes she broke down, but she took control and picked herself up again. I admire her so much for how she handled her life.

Reflecting on my own life and some horrible experiences I had which left me devastated, I noticed how I dealt with them. I remember coming out of bad relationships years ago, being in debt up to my eye balls, having some serious health scares and getting demoted in work. At the time, I was slightly dazed and very despondent for a very short time, but then I decided to make the most out of what appeared to be a bad situation. I chose all happy things instead, focused on things that would take me closer to my dreams rather than further away. I stopped the thinking of woulda, shoulda, coulda and what if? I stopped watching soaps on the tv. After all, what a waste of my time watching other people be miserable. I started reading books, and any time I went to bed at night, if my head started taking me down the path of: *my life sucks,* I would put on an uplifting cd to focus on. I would constantly be supplying my head with ways to move forward, to be positive and happy. You only need to jump on YouTube and there are millions of uplifting audios to listen to for free.

Being HAPPY is a daily choice in how you choose to deal with things. If your car breaks down, do you kick the wheel, swear at it, start panicking about being late, and get yourself really angry OR do you choose to accept you can't change what's happened, take the necessary steps to get it sorted and enjoy reading a book or looking at the views while you wait for help?

If someone puts you down or makes judgements on you, do you fight back and get nasty, get angry and defend yourself OR do you accept that it is only their perception of you, their judgement on you, not who you really are? Leave them to carry on wasting their energy on trying to make you feel bad.

If you lost your job or have been made redundant, do you chuck the towel in and say: my life sucks, I will never get another job anywhere, OR do you value yourself enough to maybe think that something better is around the corner and that it's a chance to try something new?

All choices we make will result in how we feel and how we perceive a situation as being Good or Bad.

For me, what appears to be bad I choose to see as good. Sometimes things happen out of our control and it may seem dreadful at the time but when you look back on it, you will see how much it has grown you as a person.

I remember once working at a huge radio station on a breakfast show and we were changed to another station that was really small and a lot further away for me to drive and I really didn't like the area. However, I trusted that this was happening for the bigger picture. Life had bigger plans for me. So, I was happy about the choice even though everyone else thought I was mad. What happened 6 months later after being on the other station was I got job offers all over the UK, but most importantly I got an offer to work closer to home doing a breakfast show with a radio colleague who had become my best friend. I then went on to do some tv work also. I was so happy. None of this would have happened had I not been moved from my job.

Being happy for me means making conscious choices about how I deal with situations. It's about knowing that I have a choice on if I will let something break me or make me.

So, if you're feeling unhappy, then make some different choices. Find the good in the bad, the up in the down. If you look closely enough, you will find something to be happy and grateful about even if it's just that you have managed to smile on a rainy day!

A Matter of Life or Death

"Every moment is a chance to start again, tomorrow is never given, yesterday has gone. All you have is NOW. This very moment is the only thing you can control."

How would you live your life today if you knew tomorrow was your last day on this planet? For some people that is actually a reality. Some people have terminal illnesses and that is a question many could be asked.

I often find that people are only grateful for their life when things are put into perspective for them. They lose a family member, a relationship breakdown, losing their home, basically some of life's huge traumatic experiences. What can happen after these experiences is some lose their way. Forever rehashing and reliving what they should or could have done.

Some have instant realisation and become very grateful for life but wouldn't it be great to have that wake-up call without the horrific experience?

When I had my serious car crash in which my car was crushed and set on fire, I somehow, through sheer willpower managed to drag myself out of my car, even though both my knees were broken, along with my ribs and skin wounds. Most people would see that as something quite horrible to experience and so did I at the time, but this horrific accident happened to be the best thing that ever happened to me. After being in hospital for a month, the next 12 months were spent being stuck at home not being able to walk until my legs had healed. This was a crazy time as all I could do was watch tv, being drugged up on pain killers but instead I chose to read books and get my life into check.

At the same time I was in hospital, there was another girl who had a similar experience to me in a car crash. A year later I bumped into her and her life was dreadful. Through fear she had not got into a car again; she had sunk into depression because she was stuck at home bored, she left her job because she had lost confidence with communicating to people and put on 4 stone of weight, not to mention her fiancé had left her because they were fighting all the time and she hated the scars on her legs because she said they were ugly. I know how hard it was for her, after all being stuck at home alone for 12 months is a long time to become fearful and focus on how bad your life is.

We both had the same experience but had completely different results. You see for me that accident was a wake-up call. A reality check on how lucky I was and how blessed I was to be alive. It made me do the things I had always dreamed of because I knew life was too precious to waste. I decided all the things I had dreamed of, I was going to make my reality and take bold steps into reaching my goals! I could get knocked down by a bus tomorrow. For her though, that accident was the end of life as she knew it.

I realised time is so precious. It's not to be wasted. Spend time with your friends, family, loved ones. Do the job you have always dreamed of. From that day onwards, I decided I would never do a job that felt like work again. I wanted to enjoy life in everything I did, not just my spare time. For that girl, fear of it happening again stopped her living her life. For me fear of not having a life started making me live mine better. FEAR does not have to be bad, you can also turn it into a positive.

In that time at home, I reflected on my life and realised how all the choices I had made had moulded my life. My attitude is what got me through difficult times. I love my scars on my knees. They are permanent reminders of how precious life is and more importantly that from what looked like the worst thing that could ever happen to me, was actually the best.

Are you happy with how you're living your life? If you are, then brilliant!! If not, then don't let FEAR stop you from moving forward; use it as a catalyst to create a better life for yourself. Ask yourself the question, if your life was taken away from you tomorrow would you feel like you have had the best life, OR have you just made do with what life has given you? It's our choice. What will you choose?

I Don't Have a Choice

"We always have choices, even if they don't look great, but there is always another option. Make the choice and if you don't like it, guess what? You can choose again."

Not having a choice is a limiting belief. When in a difficult situation, we can truly believe we have no way out. When the fact is we always have a choice. It may not be the one we want but it's always a step in the right direction. All choices have repercussions, BUT the beautiful thing about life is we can always make another choice. We have to make decisions on where we are right now, not based on what could or may happen in the future.

For example, let's say you were stuck in a job that made you unhappy but it paid the bills and put money on the table. You could stay in that job for life for the security of it, but if you were unhappy, then what would be the point? You may convince yourself that it's the only way because you have played out in your mind all the worse-case scenarios and consequences of leaving that job. Including, *that you have no choice but to stay just to survive,* so you choose to stay put. You choose to stay stuck.

You could choose to look online for another job; you may take the step to another job and hate it, your worse-case scenario could actually play out for you right in front of your eyes.

Again, that's when you make another choice. You just keep choosing till you find what you really want and what makes you happy. Choice is the most wonderful gift we have, if we use it wisely. When people say to me that they're not going to make a choice, they are just going to wait and see what happens, they are in fact still making a choice by default. For just leaving it up to chance is giving your control to others to make it for you.

I recall a time when my husband had a great job as a mortgage advisor. He never did it for the love but because the money was good. He didn't really like the job that much but the money was good so he stayed put in a high demanding job that stressed him, then he got made redundant. He had to get a job to cover the bills; he took a huge pay-cut and chose a career which he absolutely loved in the end. This forced him to re-evaluate his life and start looking for something he really enjoyed.

The moral of the story is — if you stay somewhere where you are not happy, it's unlikely things will get better, unless of course you choose to be happy in what you do. Unfortunately, many people struggle to be happy doing something they don't like therefore make a different choice. Choose another choice till you find the right fit.

Shoulda Woulda Coulda

Shoulda, woulda, coulda is one of the main things that holds many people back.

We live in a world of amazing opportunities which is fantastic but also means we can often put high expectations on ourselves. Not only in jobs, businesses, missed opportunities, relationships, health... pretty much every aspect of our lives.

We can look back thinking, if only I had done this, I should have taken more care of my health, should have gone to college...the list is endless.

We all can feel on some level that we could or should have done some things differently or dealt with them in a better way. This can often leave you feeling that in some way you have missed out, messed up and just done the wrong thing. We just generally beat on ourselves!

It can be a heavy burden and one that needs letting go of with immediate effect as it has no benefit whatsoever.

When I was younger and traveling around Australia, I was a singer and would often enter competitions or sing on karaoke.

At that time, I had a burning ambition to be a singer but the reality was I was just not ready. In a period of a year I got a approached by 3 different very well-known recording labels but I just didn't see it through or something would could up that prevented me from attending the meetings. Life was crazy busy and I was having way too much fun, working and traveling around Australia.

For years after this, I would beat myself up. When back home to the UK and normal life had resumed, I then realised what I had missed out on. I had had the opportunity to do my one dream but had missed out on it.

After this time passed and after watching some friends become famous, I realised it wasn't all it was cracked up to be.

In fact, I watched some of those friends go onto have successful lives however, being very unhappy which led them to depression.

As it turned out, my dream was about to change. Upon a visit to see some extended family, I was told by a psychic to keep my eyes open as they could see me entering the world of radio within the month.

This was something I hadn't even thought about but became very intrigued. After leaving that trip, and heading home, I heard an advert on the radio auditioning across the UK for 'radio presenter wanna-be's' which I thought was a huge coincidence. I went along with no experience or knowledge of this industry whatsoever but was very excited.

Over the next few months, thousands of people went through the audition process, many already with degrees, experience and already professionals. I was literally just having fun and enjoying the process.

I got down to the final 8 on a national mainstream radio station and ended up with a job from them. After that, it became my new passion so approached a local station and they had heard me so gave me a promotion job which eventually led to having my own breakfast show.

The reason I share this with you is that the Universe ALWAYS has your back; it is never too late and when one door closes, it's true…another door opens.

Our role is to be open. To let go of what *could have been* and be receptive to the world bringing new and better things our way.

It's not one strike and you're out. God/source has your back 'always' and is ready and waiting to give you your next best step.

It's about keeping your eyes and ears wide open. Close the door on what may have been and be ready for what could come next.

It could be brought to you in many ways… like me: an advert on the radio, a new connection, someone you meet on the train…

When you put the intention and expectations that good things are coming your way and be open to seeing them rather than beating up on yourself, you will find new chances and opportunities arise in every moment.

When you have fun and focus on feeling good rather than stressing out about the outcome, you raise your vibration to a more positive one, therefore attracting more positive vibes your way.

It's Ok to Not be Ok

Often when people are on their journey in life, trying to make changes and things better, we can encounter many things that are out of our control. The only thing we can control is our own mind and how we decide to respond to situations around us.

Learning to let go is the biggest gift you can give yourself.

You have heard the saying 'have the strength to change the things I can and except the things I can't'? There is much truth in this; we only have control over ourselves, that's it! Simple. We cannot change or make anybody do what we want. We also can't always change people's personal circumstances, like get them a better job, more money, better health and so on.

We can only be the best that we can be when we are with those people who need help and then let that go when we leave. Thinking and worrying does not benefit anyone, ever.

When I say, 'it's ok to not be ok', it's something we have to allow for ourselves and for others. We can't, as much as we would like to, always fix things for others and sometimes we can't, in that moment, even do it for ourselves.

We all fall apart, have shit days in every area of our lives and all we want to do is cry and curl up into a ball, but we don't often feel we have the right to do so. In fact, we go as far as to say to ourselves, 'I should be better, I know better, there are people in worse situations than me'.

We all need to give ourselves acceptance. So, if we want to fall apart or feel the need to, it's actually ok to. To release that energy, get it out of the system. Stay in bed all day, go for a walk, take a long soak in the bath and throw a pity party.

We are souls in a body, learning and experiencing new things every day. This is normal. This is life. Just because you have a hard time and fall apart does not make your value anything less. In fact, it makes you stronger because you give yourself permission to not be ok. To have that time out and then when you have, you can pull yourself back together again.

Learning to love yourself, as you would another, is the biggest gift to give yourself.

If someone you loved dearly was not ok, you wouldn't verbally abuse them and give them grief. You would love them, take care of, tell them to take time out, treat them, make life easier for them.

Now is the time to do that for yourself without any guilt whatsoever.

When you take care of yourself first, you can take care of others. On an aeroplane, they always tell you to put your mask on first before helping others. If you don't, you're not much use to anyone and less likely to help save lives.

It's the same in life. Unless you're good to you first, you will struggle to give the best version of you to others.

Knowing that it's totally Ok, to not always be Ok is 100% Ok! Sometimes it's needed as long as you give yourself a time limit and don't make it a permanent thing.

When you fall, you take a rest, put a plaster on and then get back up! This is no different. Be kind to you.

What About the Assholes?

"I BRING YOU NOTHING BUT ANGELS"

Big pill to swallow right? That every asshole you have encountered is an angel but then that all depends on which way you look at things.

We have all been there on some level. The nasty boss, the bitchy friend, the abusive parents, the dude that cut you up in the traffic, the ignorant sales person and basically anybody who has hurt, harmed, angered, upset you in any way.

Trust me, throughout the years I put myself in a variety of dysfunctional relationships. It seemed strange from a young age that I always seemed to encounter similar relationships over and over again. After a very abusive, violent partnership when I was young, I actually tried to commit suicide.

I had put myself in relationships from the age of 13 and before the age of 20, I had already experienced some pretty horrid things.

The reality on looking back was that I had actually attracted that to me. I almost expected it to happen and so it did.

Please hear me when I say this. **I didn't ask for it** and don't believe anyone deserves it. Although, at that time, I couldn't see how to change the situations I kept putting myself in. In fact, more often than not, I kept going back for more. Crazy, I know, as who in their 'right mind' would want to put themselves in bad relationships, but therein lies the answer. I was NOT of my right mind. I had watched soaps on tv, seen it happen to people first hand in my life, so those sorts of relationships seemed my normality and the Universe delivered. I got what I thought about, in fact it just seemed to follow from relationship to another, lied to, cheated on, verbally abused and the circle was never ending.

Don't get me wrong, I don't claim to be innocent in any of this even if it seemed I was. Some of my partners were lovely humans, I just managed to pull the worst out in them and push them. And they pulled the worst out of me. My energy was so out of balance and that was the same energy I would pull from others.

These experiences have come to be my greatest gift to date and I am grateful for them. Without these relationships, I would not have figured out what I did want from relationships. We need the opposite to know what it is. As I said previously, without the dark how do you know the light; without experiencing what I didn't want, how would I know what I did; without wrong how would I know right?

You might think that is a strange way to look at things and be almost grateful for those situations but what would you suggest to someone who has gone through this? To carry on with anger, revenge, upset and hatred to those who you feel have done you wrong? Where would that get you? What it does is fill you up with resentment and holds you in a place of anger, frustration and bitterness which in turn eats you alive.

Negative thoughts you hold for someone else do nothing to them and EVERYTHING to you. Forgiving someone sets you free, not them. Moving on helps you live life to the full, not them.

Forgiving others and forgiving yourself is so powerful. Although we can't change what others do to us, we can change how we choose to deal with it.

You may have had experiences happen that you had no control over. Those things may be unforgivable, fill you with all those feelings and control your emotions.

We cannot change things that have happened to us but as we get older and become aware of the fact we have our own individual beliefs and morals, not the ones society gave us, we realise we can change how we think and feel about them. After all, holding all that hurt inside only affects you. Not the other person and the more you focus on the negative, it stops you from bringing better things your way. It keeps you in a destructive circle that will pull you down.

Choose now to take your power back. Choose to let go, choose better-feeling thoughts.

You have the power within you to do things that take you in a different direction. Once you realise you are not your past, you can think higher thoughts which create better feelings and bring a higher vibration into your life.

We may not always be able to see why certain things happen to us, especially at a young age when we're brought into a system of friends/family/teachers which don't let us be aware. We were brought into these environments without choice, just taking everything on-board around us as truth. However, they were really others' projections and their truths. We just came into them. As we wake up and become conscious that we can in fact choose our own right and wrongs, we build a new wiring in our brains, a new belief that we have created, not something we picked up from our past.

As a child, we have little control as to what happens to us, unless of course we are surrounded by people who are already awake. Often, we are brought into this world surrounded by innocent people who are also not aware of how our thoughts and feelings create situations.

It's only as we grow older that we start questioning and searching for answers about life. That's when we often start to create our own beliefs. If we don't, we stay in the same programming we have been brought up with, and likewise for the generation before. Although it is not everyone's quest to see a bigger picture, the good news is that at any time, anyone can.

They can learn to see they are not their past, and they can change their old beliefs structure at any given point.

So, whatever assholes you come across in life, be them big or little ones, there is always something you can take from them. It really is your choice how you decide to live that scenario out in your mind.

Remember you choose your thoughts. Own them. Don't let others own you.

How to Deal With Negative People

"You are what you think and who you spend your time with. Spend it around negative people and you will struggle to find the joy."

In an ideal world, it would be great to be surrounded by happy and carefree people. Once you wake up, this is most definitely something that can and will happen as even when those neg-heads turn up, you learn to deal with them differently. Plus, the added bonus is, once you start raising your vibration you will find that you will attract the same sort of people to you.

You may have heard the saying that your life represents the 5 key people you spend your time with. Take an honest and serious look at your life and who is around you now. Are these people mostly happy, forward thinking, optimists, caring, loving, people who lift you up or do you find yourself surrounded by moaners, groaners, people who put you down, always talking about the bad things on the news, gossiping?

They say we are what we eat; we're also what we speak and surround ourselves with.

I would strongly suggest that if you are surrounded by nay-sayers, people who make you feel tired and heavy, upset and even depressed, then this is not a good energy for you and would encourage you to step away as soon as possible. For the more you stay around it, the more you will bring it to you. Unless you get to a stage where it will wash over your head and not even phase you.

Easier said than done, you say. What if it is your husband, wife, daughter, son, family, close friend etc...?

This is where it comes back to you and where you put your focus; as we have said, we can't change people around us, we can only change how we react to them.

All of us experience different feelings and emotions and the Universe pairs us up, like a magnet. If you start moaning first thing in the morning, shouting at the woman who cut you up, the waitress who forgot your drink, stressing out over your boss at work, the likely chance of you to attract more of that will happen.

When you start your day with conscious intent and look at your thoughts and feelings, you can start to channel your energy in a different direction. You act on purpose as opposed to automated thoughts.

Everything is a cycle and it's up to us to break it. Nip it in the bud before it starts to get out of hand and the whole day spirals into non-stop chaos of feeling frustrated and fed up.

Every day, in fact every moment, is a chance to break the pattern. Once you start to focus your thoughts on to feel-good thoughts, you become aware of what you're actually thinking. You will find your energy vibration increases and in turn will start attracting more good situations your way. Like attracts like – so the normal negative people don't match up to your vibration. When they are in their bad mood, neg-head on your paths won't cross… when they're in their good moods, you will match, finding that you mostly get to the see the good sides connecting with you.

When I first had my wake-up experience, I became distant from many people. We just didn't match anymore.

It wasn't an intentional choice initially. I was so busy reading books, starting new classes, joining new groups and making new friends, I was like a sponge. I was so excited about life and intrigued as to how I could change it, I wanted to know everything NOW. There was no room for bad vibes; I felt alive and on fire with a passion unstoppable to learn all I could.

My vibration was so high that literally, I couldn't sleep at night because I was too excited to wake up. I just wanted to absorb more and more information and watch the miracles evolve in front of me. Every morning I would be planning what I wanted to attract into my life, be it new shoes or catch up with a friend…

As you can imagine, that was a huge shift. I had spent a good year house-bound and not being able to walk. People noticed my time change; some thought it was great and others thought I was crazy, simply too happy to be around.

The truth is, if you continue to surround yourself with negative, low vibration people, there is a low chance of improving your situation. Remember the goal is to raise your vibration and focus on good feeling thoughts. That can be hard to do when everything around you contradicts that.

Health...Is it Important?

*"Your body is a vehicle which carries your soul.
The same as your mind, filling it with positive vibes
creates better outcomes. Fill your body with
goodness and reap the rewards."*

That may seem like a silly question...is health important?

Firstly, your body is a vehicle that holds the essence of who you are. So, naturally it is good to eat well, drink plenty of water and keep yourself in good nick.

Eating well and exercising helps to release more endorphins and naturally makes you feel better so of course, that has the great effect of energising you.

In the same way if you look after your car...the more you do so, the longer it lasts. If you put good into it, good comes out. The same can be said of all things in life.

The better we are, treat things, ourselves and others, it bodes for more harmony BUT I want to focus on a slightly different angle. You see food, just like us, is made up of vibration and in a world where we are consuming more processed foods, drinks full of chemicals can make us feel tired and sluggish. Also, the products we use in us and on us can have their effects.

Always aim as close to natural is the best option. Our bodies are miracle machines. They really do adjust and take care of us.

However, a lot of research over the years for illnesses has been linked to stress! And where does stress originate from? The thoughts we hold in our mind. Yes, of course we can believe stress comes from outside factors but it's mainly how we perceive those outside factors and what we think about them affects us.

If you put yourself in/around energy that brings you down, let's be honest, you feel like shit. Let's say you love going to festivals, church…somewhere there is high, happy energy. Guess what? You feel good.

If you're facing health challenges, of course seek medical advice but again, it's about creating that good vibe.

Do and put yourself in high vibe, stress-free environments. Do things that ease the worry. Watch a comedy, go for a walk, have a bath, go on that night out. Focus on feeling good.

Feeling Good

*"When you feel good, you send out a message to the
Universe of joy, appreciation and gratitude which
in turn matches you up with even more
opportunities to feel good.
When you feel bad, the energy you send out will
bring more matches to line up with that feeling.
Remember the Universe has no preference, it just
gives you what you want, not from what you ask but
how you feel about what you're asking for."*

As you can see, the main core running through my
book focuses on feeling good and reaching for better
feel-good thoughts, seeing the best in everything,
trying to let go of the things you can't control and focus
on the only things you can.

The reason for this is because there is nothing else
that benefits in the way that this will. Waking up is
becoming conscious that the only thing you need to

control is what goes on in your own head and how you see and feel about things.

Everything else is irrelevant. You see life the way you want to see it, others are having their own experiences. You cannot get in someone's head and change them or think their thoughts for them, so the best thing you can do for yourself and others is seek to improve how you think and feel.

Only then can you attract exactly what you want into your life on a daily basis by really understanding the power you have and that you truly are part of all that is love, God energy, source, and because you are part of all that is – which is you – you are on your own side and want nothing but the very best for yourself.

Learning to say 'NO' to situations that don't serve you is a great place to start.

If you want to do something and it inspires you, then great. If you are saying 'YES' to something that you don't want, then it's time to ask the question… 'WHY'?

Are you people pleasing? Trying to make others happy? Don't want to let people down?

Learning to understand yourself and the patterns you have created is so good for you. Start asking yourself the question 'WHY' before you do things that you don't really want to do. Become conscious of your actions and seek a solution.

If your friends ask you out and you don't want to go: Why? It may be a number of reasons you need to address. It may be you don't feel good about yourself so don't want to talk to people. If that's the answer, then ask yourself, why don't you feel good about yourself? And seek resolution.

It may be you simply don't like them anymore and need to find a new circle.

There are many answers, but become conscious of your patterns and before taking any action, simply ask yourself why you are doing it. If you're doing it for joy, then awesome; if not, re-evaluate.

The Day I Met an Alien

I gave this section this title as this is just one of the experiences I had when I woke up and accepted who I really was.

I didn't speak much about this earlier in the book as I wanted to first explain to you how this was possible and how it happened.

If this book has helped you get to the stage that you can accept you are energy, God and part of all that is, then it becomes easier to understand how I came to experience some of the events that happened to me. You see, when you get into alignment with source then everything will seamlessly flow; you find that it's not your actions so much that make things happen but when you put out the right vibe, the Universe automatically lines up the same vibration experiences.

You see, not long after my car crash I became very much aware that I was made up from energy, to the point of walking in rooms and lights, tv, kettles would switch on.

At first I was scared, but when I understood the energetic connection, it made sense.

I frequently would have out-of-body experiences, where I would literally see my body in the bed. Sometimes if there was an outside distraction like a door knock or phone ring, I would literally jump back into my body so fast that my heart would be pounding.

My energy was changing so quickly that it even affected my body shape and facial features. It would not be uncommon for me to wake up and look like someone else, more often than not it was a family member. I seemed to take on the features of whoever's energy I was focusing on at that time. The more I seemed to delve into it the crazier it got.

One evening, I was invited to a new friend's house for a night of meditation. That evening I met many different people. Some who had previously worked at Nasa. It was a conversation had with a lovely lady that brought around what would happen next.

I had told her of my experiences and to my amazement, she was not surprised. In fact, she told me she had met many people who had become, in her words, enlightened. I asked her about a number of things, of which one was aliens and asked her if she believed. At this time, I was very curious as to everything non-normal in life. She said she believed and had met people before me who had met some.

By then, I was no longer surprised by anything and could pretty much accept that 'anything goes'.

A week later, I was invited to do a talk at a wellbeing event. The talk I did was about motivation. Afterwards, a large group of people sat down to do a talk through meditation.

Whilst going through the process, I felt a large presence behind me; it was not one that scared me but made me feel very safe. On opening my eyes, sat across from me was a man and woman, in human form initially but on my coming round they were completely different. They were white, iridescent creatures, not like the ones you see in the films but almost looked like white trees. I had to slap my face as I couldn't quite understand what I was seeing and how no one else was seeing it.

For a while, I sat there shocked, then the male came over to me and simply asked, "Did you see us?" I responded, "I am not sure what I saw." We then chatted for a while. He explained to me that they were aliens, not the ones you would expect to see but what he meant was, not of this planet. I asked how come I had seen them and no one else.

He explained that because I was open, I could see higher vibrations, of which he was one. Our conversation led to me asking why he was here. He explained to me that there was a number of beings from different planets and that we were slowly destroying ours and that he was here to help. That like on Earth, you can find good and bad energies, the same could be said of other species. He informed me that they were here simply to help raise the vibration of love, go to different areas of our planet and help people understand who they were and bring more love to the planet. That at each destination they arrived, their energy would attract light seekers, those who wanted to improve life as we know it.

Now I know this may sound far out and quite unbelievable for some, but for me at that time it made perfect sense. I was not afraid at any point and was actually intrigued as to their purpose. I could fully understand why someone would want to help us, after all, we had been living an illusion for so long that we were here just existing. We had no real control but to me, anything now seemed possible. We were a society led to believe that we came here, lived, then died with no real purpose other than to just exist.

Here was someone telling me that our true nature was of God and that we are capable of turning life as we know it around.

At first, I was so excited I told many people, however as you can imagine not many believed me. In fact, due to my high energy personality, most people thought I was joking and since I had nothing to prove from this experience, it went on to be something I mostly kept to myself. After all, could you imagine how crazy people would think I was?

I knew what had happened and I had nothing to prove to anyone. All I now knew was how important it was that I brought more love into the world and played my part in raising my vibration.

In fact, part of the reason this book took so long to write was because I was aware many may see it as slightly exaggerated and would bring up loads of questions, but over the years and research done, I have come to find endless people who have experienced similar or abnormal experiences.

Not long after this was when I would start to have clairvoyant experiences. Which I later came to understand were energy experiences. This was not foreign to me. As a teenager, I was frequent to many experiences I deemed scary at the time.

Growing up, I would often have things move around in my bedroom, the bed shake and often had the experience of a man standing at the end of my bed. Obviously, this scared the living day lights out of me as at that time all I knew was what I had seen on the tv which was mostly scary horror movies about ghosts. Again, looking back, it happened through my teenage years, mostly when my energy was all over the place with hormones. Now I can see that my energy was crazy! I was going to attract all sorts.

It only became apparent to me what that was when I understood that everything was made up of energy. In our time and other places as well.

My experience was now completely different. I had more of an understanding and realised that what I was picking up on was people's current vibration and what they were bringing in to it.

I now found that whenever I met anyone I was constantly picking up their life situation and would be bombarded with messages from other realms for people…but that's a whole other book!

This went on for some time, in fact till I decided to have children. At which point I decided that part of my life was to be put on hold whilst I spent time at home bringing up my 2 children.

This is actually a very important point to make here. Just because you wake up, it doesn't mean that life is 100% perfect all the time.

In fact, after having my children there was a time that all the magical experiences almost became a memory. I stepped back into the illusion of life and started playing out old patterns again.

I almost went back to sleep; don't get me wrong, life was great but my focus prior to the children had been on me and being able to spend large amounts of time dedicated to research and experiments. Having two children close together, I got caught up in time and the lack of it. I was either sleeping, feeding or cleaning. Which was great, I was experiencing being in the moment with the children but I certainly was not setting daily intentions, meditating and being in a high vibration. I was not directing my intention and after a while slipped back into mind thinking rather than focusing on feeling good.

I had put so little effort into creating thoughts about the future as I was caught up in 'now'.

As a result, the time came where we ended up with struggles. My mind took over and panic set in. My husband was made redundant, we were fighting all the time and life no longer felt magical. In fact, the opposite of everything I had experienced. All the daily miracles seemed to be consumed with me just wanting to sleep. Even to the point when my health visitor thought I may have post-natal depression. I just laughed. I couldn't even comprehend how she could say that. After all, as far as I was concerned, I knew everything to prevent that, so how could that happen to me?

Herein lies the next most valuable lesson.

100% Not Perfect, Is Perfect

"My idea of perfect is a blissful soak in the bath; yours could be eating a cheeseburger and fries. Neither one of us is wrong. It's in the eye of the beholder."

Bear with me, as this may sound slightly crazy. You see for most people, they think/believe that when you awake/reach enlightenment, that life is just one big party!

And I would agree: yes it is! Just not in the way that most people perceive that. Now, if you are fortunate to be able to sit in a field for the rest of your life and purely meditate, then maybe you could hold that high vibration BUT what would be the point of that? You came here for the experience, you can float around as much as you like when you leave your physical body but for the time being, you are here on this planet to experience life on every level.

This is an area I feel most people come unstuck. So busy trying to create the 'perfect life' that they are

76

constantly on the lookout for more. Now that's great, I strongly encourage everyone to want more, achieve more, strive for more but not at the detriment of feeling unfulfilled, desperate, constantly seeking complete perfectness!

This was my lightbulb moment. In the realisation of how amazing my life had become and then to find myself back where I started was a shocker. A real slap in the face.

From being queen hippy dippy, there I was again...just a different situation experiencing all manner of challenges; no sleep, depressed, fighting with my partner, struggling for money and the list went on...

After all, if my life was not the perceived 'perfectness' all the time, then how the hell was I going to help or teach others?

This was a real low for me, I felt like a hypocrite. How could I go from all those amazing experiences, having the dream radio/tv job, winning holidays and cars, having children, finding the perfect partner. Creating awesome miracles every day, speaking with God and to now being back down.

This really did play on me. In fact, it scared the shit out of me.

Initially I couldn't comprehend how this had even happened but then it hit me. I had not been focusing on feeling good or putting intentional good feeling thoughts out there.

I had stepped back into the illusion of life.

I had started sleep walking through life again.

I had become that wrapped up in doing the best for my children, I had forgot that doing the best for me was also the best for them.

I had been focusing and worrying...had they ate enough, slept enough, was I a good enough mum/wife? This was a whole new territory for me and I completely lost sight of who I was.

I had literally started living from my mind again, not in the moment. I was back to sleep walking. Just like that. I had become unconscious and started doing, thinking old patterns. Listening to others' opinions, how I should do this and that.

Over a period of time and being in hospital with the children I had put myself right back into the illusion. Everything seemed like a distant memory and even though I knew how to change it, I just couldn't seem to find a place to start. The more I complained, the worse things seemed to get.

I didn't have the time to meditate, go for a swim or even brush my hair or wipe the sick off my clothes, never mind try to feel good.

In fact, I felt that low and created all manner of craziness in my life, just this time it was mostly negative.

The good news was I could see it, I just couldn't believe I had let myself get that far down.

What happened next was the start of my wake-up call. AGAIN.

I literally cried for help AGAIN. I cried until I couldn't feel my face or body. It was like I was breathing through my skin. This time it was in disbelief that as much as I should know better, I was angry with myself for not even seeing I had reverted back.

I shouted at God... "What are you doing to me?" The answer I got back was, "What are you doing to yourself?"

At this point I knew what to do.

I literally surrendered from myself. I realised that once again I had been trying to control things out of my control. That I had been trying to do things out of action rather than focusing on my energy and trusting that the Universe had my back.

I said to God then and there…I don't know what I want or where I want to be. In fact, the only thing I do know is that from all my experiences, I had come to realise that we were all one and that at that time my energy sucked and I needed help from the Universe in changing it.

I needed to stop trying to DO with actions and trust that God/the Universe had my back and seeing as I was back in my mind I needed to get out of my own way and get back in alignment with source. As if me, in my mind didn't know what to do, surely God, me out-of-my-mind would!

After all, I am part of God so who knows what's best for me other than God…part of me, my higher self.

I literally said that: I hand myself over. To be of service to others, (others are also part of you) and I want the best for everyone involved, whatever that may be.

No asking for this or that, literally…what is best for everyone.

For the best everyone is will also be the best for me. For I am part of all that is, was and ever will be.

Dramatic I know, but I had literally got to the end of my tether AGAIN. I simply did not know what I wanted anymore. I had spent the previous number of years getting everything, that I had become well aware that as magical as it was, here I was again in a difficult situation.

What happened the week to follow was very interesting, although I nearly missed the signs by focusing on what I THOUGHT I should be doing. Instead of focusing on how I was feeling and changing that.

I then decided to step back and trust 100%. I kept my eye out for signs and followed. The Universe ALWAYS gives you the answers, the question is, are we watching for them?

Slowly but surely, I started paying attention again. The signs started to come thick and fast. One day I was sat on the sofa and my little boy walked for one of the first times. In doing so, he brought me a magazine over. I very kindly took it and said thank you, then put it to one side. He kept bringing it to me until eventually I saw an advert jump out at me looking for honest and ambitious people.

I made the call and spoke with a lady called Julie who had a work-from-home opportunity. We met and it seemed very exciting but, I decided it wasn't for me.

A month later, I was surprised nothing had turned up. No signs...nothing. Or at least no signs I paid attention to. I asked God again, "Where are you?"

The following day, the phone rang and it was Julie again...did I want to consider the opportunity in more detail?

I was excited about it, but really didn't believe it was something I wanted to do. I didn't believe it was my calling, however after ignoring God the first time, I thought I better go along with it. After all it may just be a stepping stone to a direction I was meant to go in and in the meanwhile if it helped pay the bills, then what did I have to lose?

The result of that was a business I went on to do for several years, earning me a dream income and most importantly, helping others. The more I followed the signs, the more 'great things' came my way.

From that business, we managed to build our dream home, have many luxurious holidays and more importantly to me, be at home with my kids. Life was one big miracle. In fact, it was just like a dream. What I learnt was to let go of my expected outcome. Let go of the way I wanted things to transpire and to simply trust in God to bring even bigger and better things my way.

At the same time, I became involved with my local church, where I got to meet the most amazing people and learn more about Jesus and what he stood for as a person. I saw a different view to what I had previously understood as a child which was fire and damnation.

I actually studied the principles of what Jesus stood for, which was unconditional love. Everything always comes back to love.

I learnt some incredible lessons along the way.

What was the lesson? What did I learn? That even when things don't seem perfect, they actually are. Even when you're down, there is always a way back up and that everything is always happening perfectly, even when it seems not to be.

That's the real success in life. When through trials you know that for every down there is an up, without the down how could you come back up?

The real perfection is in knowing that life is full of experiences, good and bad but when you reach a place of being awake, you can see that. You can, even in the darkest of places know that the Universe has your back and is always working in your favour. Your job is to watch for the signs, look for the joy and follow the steps to getting there.

When you reach this space, life truly is a constant blessing, even if it doesn't seem like it in that moment. Things truly are always working out for you.

Take a look back at hardships from the past. For many, you will be able to find a positive now, even if not at the time it was happening.

You may have heard this story before but it is one of my favourites.

The end of the world is here and everywhere is flooded. A man said, "I do not fear because God will save me." As the floods got worse, a boat turned up and they told him to jump in. He refused and claimed God was coming to save him. As it got worse, a helicopter turned up and offered him safety. Again, he said, "No, God will save me."

Eventually he drowned and as he spoke with God he said, "God I waited for you, but you did not save me...Why?"

God replied, "I sent a boat and a helicopter, what more did you want?"

It's a reminder to always be open to the signs and even when times seem dark, things are always working out for you.

The Best for Everyone

"If I was to tell you that everyone you meet is you,
that when you hate, love, judge, criticize, be kind,
be giving, be jealous...that you are, in effect,
attacking OR loving yourself?
By asking for the best for everyone, you are in fact
also asking for the best for yourself."

Often, when we focus on wanting something, we want it for ourselves and in a particular way.

Understanding the following will help you receive things quicker into your life.

We say, 'ask and it is given' and it is ALWAYS given. The challenge can then come if it doesn't come in the way we want or expect it. This is where complete trust that the Universe has your back comes into play.

The Universe has bigger and better ways of bringing things to you. More often than not, in more exciting and spectacular ways that you simply couldn't imagine.

It can see every which way and every possible outcome for you.

Your job is to let it do the work and step out of its way but be ready to openly receive the signs.

For example, in your head you may want a promotion at work, doing everything within your power to receive it. You ask for it, and then don't get it. You may wonder what went wrong, the Universe didn't deliver your desires! Then, you think it simply does not work however, what you couldn't have seen was that the Universe was preparing something even better, with more pay, closer to home, less hours. The key is not to tie your desires to a specific person or thing but to ask for the end outcome of what that situation will bring.

For example, you may want the promotion because you believe it will bring more money, time, stress-free, etc.

Your job is to focus on exactly just that, not the specific job. Your thoughts should be: 'I would like a job I like with ease, that gives me more time, endless money, great holidays, great car', and then let the Universe line it up for you.

I remember a time this happened for me regarding my career in radio. I desperately wanted to do the breakfast show where I worked. I did extra hours at work and got passed over for promotions on many occasions. It was not until after my wake-up call that I actually got the job.

Eventually I took a step back and offered it up.

I said, 'I would like to do a breakfast show, with someone fun, to laugh every morning and however that happened would be for the best for everyone involved'.

The following morning I went into work, got called into the office and was demoted. I was taken off a huge radio station and put on one I really didn't like, along with the rest of my co-workers who were all absolutely devastated. It was a smaller station, less pay, less listeners and much further travel for all of us. It was a real blow. However, I knew full well, as harsh as it seemed, that the Universe had bigger plans although, at the time it really did not seem like it. I had to have full faith that things would work out and go along with the plans.

It actually turned out better than I thought and I didn't hate it as much as first perceived but I plodded along knowing that there must be a reason for this change.

As it turned out, 3 months later I got offered not one, but 3 breakfast show jobs at different radio stations. The best part was, one of them was with a previous co-worker who was my best friend. I ended up on that job for 8 years. Fun and giggles every day with one of the most amazing people in the world. It never felt like a job but just fun every day. The Universe could not have made it more perfect for me if they tried.

Letting go of a specific outcome tied to a particular person or situation just slows down the process.

Asking for what you want and the best outcome for everyone involved allows the Universe to deliver quickly and align the right people up with you.

I Want to be a Millionaire

"Having 'THE DREAM' is not what brings you happiness, it's the journey to that dream you came here for, the end result is just the cherry on top."

Wanting to be a gazillionaire is not a bad thing however, let's look at the reasons why most people think or believe their life will be better if they are.

Often, when focusing on what you want from life, be it the dream house, perfect partner, shiny car... whatever that it is for you, it's the fact that you BELIEVE that you want those things because it will make you feel good. You don't want things for the sake of it. You want that job, partner, car, house, holiday etc...because you believe by getting it, it will make you happy. I have been there myself where I have thought winning the lottery would be the answer to my prayers.

But when you understand you are just heading for the feeling those things will give you, you can really start to shake your life up.

Many people take drugs, illegal and legal because of feeling better; many addictions are brought about by it. The need for feeling good creates many habits. Drinking, smoking, drugs, relationships, shopping and the list is endless.

Many habits created for one reason only: FEELING GOOD!

The problem with this is most are short-lived. Many people do these in the aim or hope that they will be happy and although these things can and do temporality make people happy, they only fill a whole.

Using these things actually allows them to control your feelings instead of you controlling them.

I am not knocking any of these things, in fact I can see exactly why we use them. Who doesn't want to feel good, however these are short-lived, resulting in often feeling worse after the come down.

More and more people are looking and needing to find ways to feel good using outside factors, when really the best way to feel good is go inside. To realise that the reason you want and do most things is to feel good.

WHAT does feeling good look like to you? Being at ease, stress free, more holidays, more time, more fun, more inspiration and excitement???

What if you choose to feel good first? What if, rather than worry about how you can get/have/be/do which will make you feel good…just feel good anyway.

Why? It's because feeling good is what brings more feeling good about. You don't actually need anything to feel good.

It's a choice and you can do it now. How do I feel good without the end outcome in front of me? It's a matter of choosing those thoughts that bring about that feeling.

Rather than being aware you don't have your perfect partner right now, and your thoughts are focused on feeling lonely...you're wasting energy. Sit and imagine the opposite. Visualise what it will feel like. What does that feel like to you?

Safe, fuzzy, warm: create those feelings with your thoughts. Instead of being aware you don't have that partner and feel alone, frustrated and think about that, choose to think of the opposite.

Spend your normal 'WORRY' time as 'FANTASY TIME'. Don't sit there fretting and worrying, it benefits no one. Understand this: every second you spend on anything negative does not help you or anyone. Can you see that?

Anytime something negative pops into your head recognise it. The sooner you recognise and say, "Thank you because I know you're trying to find a solution but worrying won't fix it." Don't get angry at your thoughts; they are only trying to help you from the past data or programming you have. They are not against YOU, just outdated information, which is mostly of no use.

Then nip it in the bud and try a little at a time to think something better, daydream, fantasize ... really get lost in good-feeling thoughts because even if you don't believe in what I say, what do you have to lose? Better an hour in bed thinking and feeling great things than an hour of worry over something you have no control of. Which makes sense to you?

The Days of Creation at its Best

We will talk more about this in the chapters to follow, but here I want to share my personal experience of some of the things I attracted to me and how they came about.

One of my personal favourites was winning a car on The Price Is Right and how I planned it.

Six weeks prior to being on the game show, I had been coming home from work late in the evening. About six miles from home and just before a roundabout, my car literally conked out. The gear box was stiff and hard to move and was slowly but surely getting worse but that was not the problem...my exhaust actually fell off.

I had been wanting a new car for a while, and this was a way of the Universe bringing it to me.

As I sat waiting for the road service guys to appear, instead of feeling distraught and angry, I actually laughed to myself recognising that I was clearly going to need that new car sooner rather than later as to fix the car would be more expensive than the car itself.

As I got driven home and my car was taken away, I knew that better things were on their way.

The following weeks I had to get lifts to work. I didn't have the funds immediately to buy a new car, so I offered it up to the Universe to take care of it.

As people asked me: where was my car and what was I going to do, I would simply reply with, "I have a new car on its way." I never went into detail with anyone about it.

About four weeks later, I received a random call from a friend. She said, "Irene, I remember years ago that you said as a child you used to love watching The Price Is Right. Well, I have a coach-load of people going to be part of the audience and two of them have dropped out. Would you like to take their place?"

I said yes and got very excited that this could be where I would get my car. The day came where myself and Mum drove to the show. On the way, I recall speaking with my mum, telling her I was going to win a car. I even talked about the colour of it. I was so excited and sure that this was the day. We went along to Granada TV studios and the excitement was unreal… I kept saying to myself in my head… 'Irene Remelie, come on down'.

We sat all day on the set watching it being filmed and all of a sudden, the day was over. I was shocked and looked at my mum. "Oh well, my car must be coming a different way. We were just about to leave when the producer shouted out from the stage to the audience. He said that ten people had dropped out of the audience for tomorrow's show, could anyone come back again and bring ten people with them? I immediately said Yes, and the following day turned up with some of my family. I knew this was it…as each contestant got called up, I jumped up with excitement. I knew my time was coming and then I heard my name...

As you can imagine I nearly wet myself, not so much because I was on the show, but because I could see the law of attraction working right in front of my eyes!

The best part was that cars were normally ever won in the grand final, not in the smaller games. The game I played was bursting a balloon on a dart board. I bagged myself 3 darts and near-enough missed the board.

As I chucked my final dart, people said they could see me muttering to myself. I was actually saying to the Universe...'Thank you for my car'...I burst the balloon and won myself a brand new car!

The unfolding of how I got this car was awesome. The key to it was complete trust and faith that the Universe would provide.

When my car broke down, I could have been pissed off. Having to get lifts and not having the money to buy a new one could have made me frustrated and angry but through it all I maintained that God had my back and would bring it to me. I did not know how BUT knew that it would.

I talk in this book how I came to be in radio but one of my favourite manifestations was a tv show I got to do with a lady who is now one of my very best friends.

I decided I would like to try my hand at some tv presenting. At this point I was attracting all sorts of things, from shoes, to owning my own house, to free food and all sorts of little and big things. I thought, why not some tv work...

I had become very confident with manifesting things and was so excited about life that I felt like a magician. I remember telling some of those close to me, "I am going to do some tv work."

Again, when they asked what, I replied with, "It's a surprise."

About two months later I got a random call from a friend I used to work with who had a tv show presenting solo.

She said they were wanting two people to host it and were going to hold auditions, however she had put my name forward to the producer who would like to meet me.

The auditions never happened as on meeting him I was offered the job.

Putting the intention out there and trusting it will come in its own time and way allows it to come quicker.

Ask for SIGNS

We have talked about looking out for signs from the Universe but you can also ask for them. In the early stages, I was very indecisive and struggled making big decisions. Then when I knew the Universe was working with me, I would ask for specific results.

You often hear of people who take signs of feathers or butterflies from their loved ones who have passed over from physical form. This was no different.

When I was in full flow, decision-making became easier. I would pick a yes and a no answer for my questions.

I really put it to the test by picking really bizarre ones. I remember a time when I needed to make a decision about a relationship and what direction I should go in. Driving along in my car, I announced out loud that if the answer was 'yes' then I would like to see a zebra, if 'no' then a lion. I expected the answers to come in many ways. It could be on a billboard, a conversation, a picture on something I bought from shop, a necklace or tattoo, basically in any way shape or form that it came up.

On this occasion it happened so quickly that I nearly crashed my car through shock. Driving along the motorway, I was just about to come off at a roundabout, when low and behold there was an actual REAL zebra in a field… it turned out the circus was in town and they were letting it have a run in the field.

Another time, I asked for a sign of a flower…a lily (this was when I was in Australia and they were out of season and hard to come across). The following day when we arrived at our holiday home, as we walked up the path I could see a big sign on the door saying, 'Lily Cottage'.

I used this a lot to begin with until I trusted my own intuition more. Sometimes the signs would be almost instant and other times it could be days, even weeks but I always trusted either way that the timing was perfect and that if I didn't get an answer, then I didn't need to make a decision right now.

At first when I tried it I thought it was coincidence but the more bizarre my requests got, they still kept coming.

Human Energy Fields and Chakras

We have talked about energy from one standpoint but one of the main ways this process is widely accepted is through something known as chakras.

I have put this part in the book for those who want a deeper understanding, this may explain for you in more detail. You do not need to know all of this for the purpose of this book, however I appreciate some may want more information and have added it purely for those who do.

I certainly did not understand any of this for my wake-up process; only as I researched and trained as an energy healer did I see how people could relate to it.

The Chakras

This is a brief introduction to the human energy field and chakras.

As we have discussed, everything in the Universe vibrates and all living organisms have a vibrating energy field. All living cells, tissues, and organs, and the body as a whole generate measurable electromagnetic fields, called subtle energy fields or bio-fields, allowing our life-force energy to flow uninterrupted. Blockages or imbalances on any level of our energy field may interrupt this flow of life-force energy and may ultimately lead to illness and the experiences we have.

Many people choose to use certain techniques which may help to dissipate and 'clear' this blocked energy and rebalance the overall energy field of the body, which may then create a healthy environment within the body for self-healing to take place.

The energy created by our emotions, thoughts and mental attitudes and perceptions permeate via the chakras to our cells, tissues and organs ultimately affecting our physical body. The human energy field has areas where the energy tends to be more concentrated and focused. These areas are called chakras. Chakras are spinning vortexes or energy points located in and around our physical body. Through these we receive, transmit and process energy, which interacts as one holistic system.

There are seven main chakra centres: The Base chakra, The Sacral chakra, The Solar Plexus chakra, The Heart chakra, The Throat chakra, The Third eye chakra and the Crown chakra.

It is important to understand what each chakra represents, where they are located, and what emotions are related to each chakra.

It is important that should you wish to know more about chakras that you take your own time to discover in more detail.

Emotions are normal but suppression of the emotions may be a factor in physical and emotional ill health.

Each chakra governs a particular area of the body and can have an influence on the related organs, glands, tissue and cells in that location.

The word 'chakra' is derived from the Sanskrit word meaning 'wheel'. Literally translated from the Hindi it means, 'Wheel of Spinning Energy'. A chakra is like a whirling, vortex-like, powerhouse of energy. Within our bodies, you have seven of these major energy centres and many more minor ones.

You can think of chakras as in the invisible energy we have talked about and how we can help get into alignment.

The energies are charged and recharged, balanced and drawn out through contact with the stream of universal energy in the atmosphere in much the same way that your home is connected to a central power source within a city – the only difference is that this cosmic energy source is free.

Imagine this, a vertical power current rather like a fluorescent line that runs up and down the spine, from the top of the head to the base of the spine. Think of this as your main source of energy. The seven major chakras are in the centre of the body and are aligned with this vertical 'power line'.

Chakras connect your spiritual body to your physical one.

They regulate the flow of energy throughout the electrical network (meridians) that runs through the physical body. The body's electrical system resembles the wiring in a house. It allows electrical current to be sent to every part, and it is ready for use when needed.

Sometimes chakras become blocked because of stress, emotional or physical problems. If the body's 'energy system' cannot flow freely it is likely that problems will occur. The consequence of irregular energy flow may result in physical illness and discomfort or a sense of being mentally and emotionally out of balance.

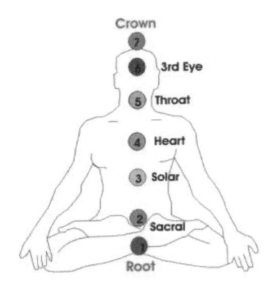

This image shows where the main chakras are located in your body. Below is a brief explanation of what they are.

Chakra 7 – The Crown

Its colour is violet and it is located at the top of your head. It is associated with the cerebral cortex, central nervous system and the pituitary gland. It is concerned with information, understanding, acceptance and bliss. It is said to be your own place of connection to God, the Chakra of Divine purpose and personal destiny. Blockage can manifest as psychological problems.

Chakra 6 – The Third Eye (or Brow chakra)

Its colour is Indigo (a combination of red and blue). It is located at the centre of your forehead at eye level or slightly above. This chakra is used to question the spiritual nature of our life. It is the chakra of question, perception and knowing. It is concerned with inner vision, intuition and wisdom. Your dreams for this life and recollections of other lifetimes are held in this chakra. Blockage may manifest as problems like lack of foresight, mental rigidity, 'selective' memory and depression.

Chakra 5 – The Throat

Its colour is blue or turquoise and it is located within the throat. It is the chakra of communication, creativity, self-expression and judgement. It is associated with your neck, shoulders, arms, hands, thyroid and parathyroid glands. It is concerned with the senses of inner and outer hearing, the synthesising of ideas, healing, transformation and purification. Blockage can show up as creative blocks, dishonesty or general problems in communicating ones needs to others.

Chakra 4 – The Heart

Its colour is green and it is located within your heart. It is the centre of love, compassion, harmony and peace. The Asians say that this is the house of the soul. This chakra is associated with your lungs, heart, arms hands and thymus gland. We fall in love through our heart chakra, then that feeling of unconditional love moves to the emotional centre commonly known as the solar plexus. After that it moves into the sexual centre or Base chakra where strong feelings of attraction can be released. When these energies move into the Base chakra we may have the desire to marry and settle down. Blockage can show itself as immune system, lung and heart problems, or manifest as inhumanity, lack of compassion or unprincipled behaviour.

Chakra 3 – The Solar Plexus

Its colour is yellow and it is located a few inches above the navel in the solar plexus area. This chakra is concerned with your digestive system, muscles, pancreas and adrenals. It is the seat of your emotional life. Feelings of personal power, laughter, joy and anger are associated with this centre. Your sensitivity, ambition and ability to achieve are stored here. Blockage may manifest as anger, frustration, lack of direction or a sense of victimisation.

Chakra 2 – The Sacral (or Navel chakra)

Its colour is orange and it is located between the base of your spine and your navel. It is associated with your lower abdomen, kidneys, bladder, circulatory system and your reproductive organs and glands. It is concerned with emotion. This chakra represents desire, pleasure, sexuality, procreation and creativity. Blockage may manifest as emotional problems, compulsive or obsessive behaviour and sexual guilt.

Chakra 1 – the Base (or Root chakra)

Its colour is red and it is located at the perineum, base of your spine. It is the chakra closest to the Earth. Its function is concerned with earthly grounding and physical survival. This chakra is associated with your legs, feet, bones, large intestine and adrenal glands. It controls your fight or flight response. Blockage may manifest as paranoia, fear, procrastination and defensiveness.

Information on the chakras is readily available online. The above has been derived from my learnings with www.energyhealingtrainingcourse.com and is a simple overview of the chakras to help readers understand the importance of human energy fields.

Access Energy

We have spoken in great detail about energy throughout this book. How we are all made up of it. How we are all connected by it and how it runs through everything we do and are.

In this chapter I want to talk about ways to help you raise your vibration and give you tools to help.

Now you understand how it all works, here are some practical steps you can take daily to turn your life around and have access to all you wish to create.

Energy can be changed and shifted in a number of ways.

A lot of these can be done with our five senses alone, which help us to raise our vibration: seeing, hearing, tasting, touching and smelling. All five of these are intertwined.

SEEING –

We spend every day using this sense to experience and perceive what is going on around us.

A way to make sure you encounter better experiences is to make wiser choices of what you pay attention and focus to.

It is time to make better choices based on how they make you feel. Do you watch the tv? Read newspapers? Scroll through pointless Facebook posts? Where is your attention?

When I woke up, I actually couldn't watch tv due to the amount of negativity that quite frankly I couldn't control.

I used to watch soaps and love them, often even crying at them as I got dragged in emotionally to the characters in the scenes, often relating to them and bring similar experiences into my own life.

Pay attention to what you watch and choose only good-feeling activities.

If you like watching tv, choose those things that leave you feeling positive, not drained. Find things that educate and make you feel uplifted; stay away from situations you can avoid that will affect how you think and feel.

HEARING –

Ask yourself what do you listen to? Who do you listen to?

How does it make you feel?

Are you listening to horror stories on the radio or do you choose your favourite song? Are you listening to people who moan, gossip and put you or others down?

Choose differently. Pick those things that bring you joy.

Pick music, songs, audio, even the birds in the park or the ticking clock. Again, things that uplift you, not deflate you.

TASTING –

Do you know that most people eat so quickly, they don't even taste their food? Taste is a great pleasure. It is the time to truly take things slower; by all means eat and drink the things you love, BUT actually take the time to taste and think about each bite you take, really savour everything that enters your mouth. Experiment with new foods and be grateful for what you put in your body.

The next time you eat, pay total dedication to it. Have no distractions, no tv, radio or talking. Just pay pure focus on every mouthful. Chew every piece of food. I can assure you that taste will have a whole new meaning.

SMELL –

Smell can bring so many joyful feelings about. Your favourite perfume, the flowers in the breeze, the fresh sea air or cut grass. Smells create great feelings. If need be, put fresh flowers in your house, take the time to smell all the wonderful things around you.

Smell heightens the senses and brings around pleasure feelings.

TOUCH –

Touch is an incredible gift. To be able to feel everything: your clothes, a loved one, a pet, a flower, water, sand. Absolutely EVERYTHING.

These all seem like really simple things. They are. Experiencing God and finding the answers and connection was never meant to be hard.

By focusing on these simple things, it brings you into the moment, into the now and out of your mind chatter.

The more present in each moment you become, the more aware of your connection to God/source is felt.

The key to becoming awake is becoming more present in every moment, knowing that when your mind starts to chatter, you can stop the thoughts by changing the direction of where they are heading.

Using your senses to become more in the moment helps you to wake up and it really is that simple.

If you pay attention to these, you can literally start to see results and changes around you in a matter of days.

Meditation Made Easy

One of the best ways to connect is to meditate. When I first heard of meditating years ago, I really struggled with it. From all the readings and teachings I had found, I just believed it impossible. I almost felt like it was something incredibly hard to do. That I was never quite going to get there, but the truth for me was I was making it too hard, putting too many expectations on myself of what I should or shouldn't feel.

What I came to realise is that it is just a matter of shifting your focus and reminding myself of where I came from and connecting to it. Feeling present, getting out of my mind chatter.

When I first started meditating I used to have a fight with my myself because I couldn't stop thinking. I would literally end up arguing with myself.

When I realised that really what was important was that I felt relaxed, that I was able to recognise those thoughts without attaching feelings to them, but more importantly just watching what popped into my mind and letting it go.

All you are really wanting to do is ease the mind chatter and shift your attention to more good-feeling thoughts.

It is great to start each morning with 10 to 15 minutes of becoming aware. Put yourself in a quiet place where you will have no distractions (I set my alarm clock 30 minutes earlier than when I wake my kids).

It's nice to have a separate room but if you don't, it doesn't really matter, your bed will do just fine.

I suggest sitting up comfortably to do this. When I first started this, I used to lie down and become so relaxed I would fall back to sleep. The purpose is not to fall asleep but to shift your energy to help you create your day ahead and start it by feeling good.

Sit comfortably; you can sit in silence or focus on a clock ticking. If you find that difficult, then maybe pick relaxing music to play in the background. There are also many guided-meditations you can listen to on YouTube and other places.

The aim of this is to feel the presence of who you really are. To feel good and alive.

It's really important to have some focus, otherwise your thoughts will run away with you.

I like to start by taking 3 slow, deep breaths and counting in my mind as I take them in and out...

Breathe in: 1,2,3 and out 1,2,3. Do this around 5 times and you will find that you start to relax more and more with each breath.

I then imagine a bright light (love, God, source) coming into the top of my head and spreading down my body, into my arms, hands, fingers through my torso, hips, legs, right down to my toes...

Don't panic if your mind starts to wander, just go back to counting your breaths for focus.

You will notice that as you start to relax, you will become more aware of what is around you, you will start to feel more present in the moment and aware of your senses. In this time, you will remember you are not just your body but start to feel the energy you are made up of.

The first few times you try this may feel strange but over time it will become much easier and with practice you will feel the connection quicker and stay in a relaxed state for longer periods of time.

After those 15 minutes, you will feel more energised and in this time it's where you can start to direct your thoughts to how you want your day ahead to be.

Affirmations are good here; you may say things like: Today is going to be fun; this day will be full of ease; today I will meet like-minded people; work will flow easily and quickly...

Basically, you are starting your day on the right side of your bed as they say OR going to bed feeling excited for the next day. Also, this is the time to focus on your story which we will cover in the next chapter.

You can use this technique throughout the day, especially when you're finding yourself stressed.

You may not be able to find a quiet room and sit for 15 minutes but what you can do if you are sat at a desk or anywhere for that matter, is to stop, take some deep breaths and become present, reminding yourself you're a soul in a body, here for an experience and pull your attention away from your mind chatter and remind yourself of your intentions for the day.

The Plan

To help you get started on your journey, follow this simple process for life. That may seem like a huge step right now, so let's start with a 7-day process, which if you follow, will raise your vibration and start the shift that is needed. You will find over time that you will want to continue this for as long as you enjoy it, but let's at least aim for a week.

The fact that you have read this book will have already created massive shifts and open your mind to a new perspective, so congratulations. You already have triggered your mind and soul to start creating.

The great news is, EVERYTHING you need is FREE, your God-given right to shine and love your life. The only decision to be made is if you're ready to take the next step.

For the next 7 days, you are going to need 15/30 minutes in the morning when you wake and the same before sleep.

The reason for this is to create a clearer mind and keep yourself in connection with source.

Morning and evening are the main times people create what I call, 'The roll', where they think, ponder, worry, predict and put the energy into flow. In the morning, it's normally concerns for the day ahead, and in the evening, it's normally worrying about what has been or what will be the following day.

It is always best to try and get yourself into a relaxed state before sleep, such as a bath, reading a book...not having too many distractions happening around you.

The purpose of these 15/30 minutes is to start changing your energy and shift the pattern.

I would suggest that in this time you have something that helps you relax, maybe dimmed lighting, soft music, meditation, a burning candle.

Before you go to sleep each night, take 10 to 15 minutes to meditate as we spoke about previously.

To strengthen this process, to begin with we are going to also write your story. Once they are written you won't need to write it again unless you want to add or change things over time.

Now is where the fun work begins. Before you start this process, you will need some time to focus on what you want from your life and how you would like to feel on a daily basis.

You are going to write your story, one that can be read each evening and will help you with the visualization process when going to sleep after your meditation.

Focusing on what has been... shoulda, woulda, coulda, does not help. We are going to focus on what you want instead of what you don't.

Each night before you go to sleep, you are going to remind yourself of who you are, what you want and how you want to feel. This is individual to each person but it's important to understand what you want and how it will make you feel.

For example:

I have my dream job and it feels amazing. I feel relaxed and confident in knowing I have reached my goal. It allows me to have more free time and to go on holiday with my friends.

I wake each day feeling stress-free, relaxed and excited about the day's events and what wonderful things the Universe will align me with.

I feel confident, excited about each day and the new adventures it may bring.

I like to spend more time with my family and cooking our favourite foods; seeing everyone enjoy the meals I have cooked makes me feel fulfilled. My new car is so spacious it feels heavenly to drive. I take great comfort in knowing how safe it is and it feels exhilarating driving through the country. Our house is beautiful, the log fire keeps us warm in the evening and I get a fuzzy feeling all snug on the sofa with the ones I love. My favourite part is waking each morning looking over the balcony and seeing the trees and birds, hearing them sing and smelling the fresh sea breeze as it fills the bedroom.

I love working from home, knowing I can stay in bed longer just relaxing and revelling in how amazing this life is.

I feel blessed that I know every day, all is working out for me....

This is very brief but what I want you to understand is that this is about the feelings it gives you, not the actual outcome. We are aiming to rewire old thought patterns and create new ones.

Remember we have talked in detail about the reason you want things is due to the belief that by having them you will feel better. The purpose of writing your life story is to get the feelings that match it. It's not so important for what you want, BUT how you will feel when having it; this is what will bring it about. Create those feelings in the present moment, so don't be too specific, let the Universe bring you what is best. Instead of writing 'I want that house No 2 Rose Drive and that job at Gilbert's as the Manager', write about the feelings you believe you will have by getting them. As if it's not those specific ones that come, you can be sure it's because the Universe is lining up something better.

Keep this story by your bedside as you may want to read it, pay reference to it as you go to sleep.

When you are ready to go bed for the night, those 15/30 minutes needed to be focused on meditation, day-dreaming, feeling good and hopeful mixed in with excitement.

Before you sleep you may find this also useful to read each evening.

Before you settle down to enjoy your day-dreaming, you can also read out loud the following statement below:

Thank you for this day. I am grateful to be alive and appreciate all the wonderful experiences life has given me today.

I know that I am here on an experience. I know that I am a soul in a body and that this is a vehicle to experience all that life has to offer.

I am part of all that is. I am part of God and therefore I have the ability to live in joy and create a life of abundance.

I know that my thoughts and feelings help me to understand the next best step of direction to take me to all I wish to live.

I choose to let go of today and know right now as I go to sleep that everything is happening perfectly. That to worry about today's events has no benefit to me, only that I should let go and relax. In this moment I can do nothing to change what has passed and take comfort in knowing tomorrow is a new day and a new start.

As I go to sleep, I will take the time to focus on my breathing, feel the comfort of my bed, knowing that I have done all I can do today and that what hasn't been done now can wait till tomorrow. I am going to relax in the knowledge that I have the chance to make changes again tomorrow, safe in the knowledge that everything is working out for me.

I appreciate all that has gone before me today and rest peacefully that tomorrow is a new day full of exciting opportunities.

I am all that is. I have the power to create the changes I want and to feel good in every moment, I choose to think better-feeling thoughts. I have boundless abundance and understand that the Universe is always on my side.

Once you have read this, spend the time before you sleep focusing on those thoughts that make you feel good and day-dreaming about your story.

Each morning when you wake, before you do anything else, take the time to remind yourself of your story and spend that time enjoying those feelings before you get on with your day. Spend this time again practising your meditation.

It is important to do this, as often when we wake we can go straight into panic mode for the day.

What you want to start your day with is excitement and hopefulness.

By meditating and focusing your attention on what you do want instead of what you don't, you are raising your vibration to one that will attract more of the good experiences into your day.

You could start your morning with reading your story after meditating and setting your intentions for the day.

Good Morning

Today is a great day to be alive. Today is a new day. Today is open for all new opportunities. Today I will stay present as much as possible, being aware of all my senses and enjoying each moment. Today I will pay attention to what I choose to focus on. What I choose to see, hear, taste and feel. I will focus on good-feeling thoughts. I take joy in all the little things around me. Today I will be aware of when I start to get lost in thought that doesn't serve me, I will notice when thoughts start to take me off track and pull them back to thoughts that benefit me, I will be present and take a step back to situations as they unfold and not let them consume me.

Today I expect things to go my way and if they don't, understand there is a purpose behind it. Today I know the Universe has my back and wants me to have joy in all I do.

I expect abundance in every area, a day full of ease and flow.

I expect the Universe to bring exactly what is needed at the right time and to watch for the signs as the beautiful unfolds in front of my eyes.

Today is a great day, it's a new day. A day full of warmth and fulfilment.

To simplify:

Each morning before you start your day and every night before you go to sleep, spend 10/15 minutes meditating. Then reading your story.

In the evening as you go to sleep, you can use that time to get lost in day-dreaming about your story.

In the morning you can set your daily intentions.

What you are doing is planning your life. Most people spend all their time planning a 2-week holiday each year. Wouldn't it be even better to plan your life with the same excitement?

Access Energy Throughout the Day

Tuning into yourself and watching your feelings is a good way to gauge the situation you're in. If you're not feeling good, this is often a signal from God/your higher self that you're not paying attention and have gone off track.

If you find yourself self-sabotaging or judging others, feelings of frustration, anger, upset, any of the lower vibration feelings, then give yourself some triggers to help you get out of them. It's easy to forget who you are when these emotions grab hold, but as soon as you become aware of them, it's the perfect chance to change them.

A number of things will help you do this.

Play your favourite song, take a nap, run outside and dance/scream in the garden, go for a walk, take 10 deep breaths, pick an affirmation, jump 10 times on the spot... all these help you to shift energy quickly and break patterns.

Yes, they are simple but they need to be. It's about breaking the momentum of that thought/feeling so you can bring better ones in. You can nip them in the bud quickly and create momentum in the better-feeling direction.

The longer a feeling stays around, the more momentum it builds to bringing in more situations that match it.

You wake up in a bad mood, you can be almost certain that unless you change it, the rest of the day will be pretty pants as you attract more and more of that energy towards you.

Ask and It Is Given

As you have heard me say, everything you want is already waiting for you. In the Bible it even says, before you have asked, it's already there!

The main focus of this book has been about finding ways to feel good, to bring ease and flow into your life. To learn to let go and focus your energy in a better direction.

Once you start getting to a place where you feel less resistance and more ease, things will flow quicker into your life.

The main 4 steps to focus on are the following:

1. Ask and it is given

Anytime you experience what you don't want, it's an opportunity to see what you do want. What you DO want is offered up.

When you say, 'I don't have enough time', you acknowledge you want more time.

When you say, 'I don't like my job', part of you knows you want something different.

When you say, 'I don't like how she or he treats me', you acknowledge how you do want to be treated.

This can be said for every negative in your life. Every time you say something you don't like, the opposite can come into play.

Every negative is a way for us to see the opposite. So, don't beat yourself up when these situations show up in your life as if you could only see them as an opportunity for you to recognise they are showing up for that reason. Every day you can see who you really want to be, what you really want to experience. The next best version of you.

The downs really do have a purpose. They are not here to punish you BUT to help you find out what you really want, how you want your life to be, what you want to happen next.

I am going to use the example of someone unhappy in a job, but this whole process can be used in every single area of your life.

Say you had a job, worked 100 hours a week, were never home and overwhelmed with stress...

If you were to focus on that, talk about it, stress more about it, moan about it, think about it, slag off your boss, shout at your children because you're tired, get angry at your spouse and feel on a hamster wheel... doing all of that will only create more of that. What you put out, the Universe just says YES and brings you more of it.

If you were to see it from a positive aspect, you would see that your higher self was screaming at you, telling you that's not what you want, it's not what you like, it's not who you are.

However, the more you complain about it, the more you get of it. It's a vicious circle…but the key is to change how you feel about it.

In an ideal world you could just quit that job and leave and if you had the money to do that whilst finding another, it would be a great option to do.

However, in the world we live, the reality we face is… I can't leave my job, we need the money, it pays the bills, it puts food on the table, what if I can't find another job that pays the same… and basically all the scary thoughts that come with change.

In this instance this is where focusing on shifting your energy and feelings have the most impact.

Try to soften those feelings and ease through to feeling better whilst acknowledging you don't want that; now is the time to focus on what you do.

However, it's hard to go from feeling low to feeling high so the process it to start creating ease. Start to find better-feeling thoughts so instead of all the frustration thoughts and words, start releasing the intensity. The more you fight against something, the more you bring it about.

You could start by saying things like this to yourself: 'This job is not forever, it's ok while I look for other things, I can see that from knowing what I don't like, I can see what I do'.

'A job that's closer to home would give me more time, if I leave this job it's not the end of the world, there must be easier ways to make the same money, there are certain parts to my job I do like. I like it when I get to lead the meetings, I like it when I get time on my own, this job has given me lots of ideas I would like to take forwards, it's helped me see the way I don't like how things are done and how I could improve them'.

All these statements can start to bring ease to the situation. Now is the time to try and bring less resistance and start creating better feelings that allow you to start attracting better vibes your way.

The more you push against something, the more you bring more of it. So, the complaining, the frustration becomes more constant. The aim is to find good factors, to try and find, if only just a little, some positive factors from that situation and spend more time focusing on those thoughts.

Instead of saying: 'I hate my job, I have no time, it just sucks the life out of me', say things like: 'I am learning from this job what I don't like. It's making me realise I want more from life. I have picked up great skills from working here, from having to do everyone else's job. It's shown me what I am capable of'.

First step is to ask. Which is automatically done when you don't want something. What you do want has been lined up for you and is ready for the taking.

2. The next step is to receive.

This is now where you need to match the vibration of what you want, creating the feelings you want so you vibrate and the Universe sends you the vibrational match.

Change your thoughts, change your feelings.

This goes back to the part where we previously spoke about raising your vibration and creating those good feelings.

Spending 15 minutes meditating, listening to your favourite songs, dancing, hugging, smelling flowers, stroking your cat – absolutely ANYTHING that makes you feel even remotely a little bit of ease, feel a little bit better because the more you feel better, the easier it becomes to feel better and the better you feel, the more you become in alignment of what you do want which in this situation would be: A stress free job, nicer people to be around, more time, love of what you're doing.

1. ASK AND IT IS GIVEN
2. GET YOURSELF INTO ALIGNMENT
3. BELIEVE AND RECEIVE

Once you start to feel more ease and better, you start to create momentum in that area and things will automatically start coming your way.

Don't try to find them, rather be open to receiving them.

Pay attention as to what is happening around you and once you are aware of your emotions and feelings, follow the signs and you will be led there. Our feelings are indicators of the direction to follow. Watch out for opportunities as they unfold in front of you.

Remember they could show up in a number of ways: You may see an advert on the back of a toilet cubicle or see it in a magazine, you may be talking to a neighbour and they mention there is a new opening at their work. Be open to what is happening around you.

I remember when I first wanted to write this book but really didn't know where to start; I was getting frustrated as I simply didn't know what to do. I knew that would not benefit and that I was wasting time thinking about it so instead I knew I had to get in a good-feeling place.

I had so much work to do but knowing that working whilst feeling frustrated would only create more of that, I literally cancelled everything and headed to the spa for the day.

Whilst there I relaxed, read a book and just enjoyed all the sensations my body was having whilst swimming, in the jacuzzi and in the steam room. I spent the entire day letting go of what I thought I had to do but instead trusting that the solution was on its way. All I needed to do was get myself in a place to receive it.

I came home feeling revived and relaxed, joyous and expectant.

Later on that evening, I had a message from a friend asking how I was. I responded and asked what were they doing now, were they still working at the bank. They went on to tell me, that yes, they were but they were also doing proof-reading for medical documents. I needed just that, a proof-reader. We decided to meet up and have a chat and as it turned out she was also doing similar work to me, in fact they were setting up a coaching academy on mindfulness.

We went on to discuss so much that we were on exactly the same path. I had not only found someone I could relate to but who would also help with my book but most importantly a new friend who was into exactly the same stuff as me and who I could potentially work with in the future.

She read some of my book and was very excited by it and that gave me the confidence to pursue it even more.

A few days later I was invited to an open business meeting where everyone there was in business for themselves and shared ideas and advice. I went along to do a talk about what is in this book. Immediately, they informed me of another amazing lady who basically does everything from proof-reading to publishing.

In a matter of days, the Universe had provided me with solutions and a path. Working with Sue is how you come to be reading this book right now.

1. ASK AND IT IS GIVEN
2. GET YOURSELF INTO THE GOOD-FEELING THOUGHTS
3. BELIEVE AND RECEIVE
4. RECOGNISE THE PROCESS

It really is that simple. Now is the point as you move forward to recognise that you go through the cycle over and over again. It may not be overwhelming situations all the time but there will be things you come up against that give you the opportunity to recognise what you don't like, what your next best step is, because that's life, forever growing. Life never stops expanding and leading you to better and higher options.

It will always give you new choices, new experiences and the more you understand this cycle and learn to let go, you'll move through it quicker. The more exciting, new, fun experiences will come to you.

Point 4 is acknowledging the cycle, knowing that moving forward you can become more awake and more aware as these things happen.

Knowing that when you know what you don't want, it also shows you what you do.

Something arises in your life that causes you to sprout another desire.

Something may show up in your life that you don't want. Rather than at this point going, oh no, not again…this is crap! Recognise that it is just pointing you, gently – directing you to the next exciting chapter of your life. Go through the process.

1. ASK AND IT IS GIVEN
2. GET YOURSELF INTO ALIGNMENT
3. BELIEVE AND RECEIVE
4. ACKNOWLEDGE THE PROCESS

Time to Wake Up!

As we come to the end of this book I hope it leaves you in a better place than when it found you.

There is so much more to talk about, but for now we have covered the simple basics.

As I said at the beginning, for some, this information is not new but just a gentle reminder you have sent to yourself about who you really are. How to create those better feelings and the process we take.

For now, this is enough information to take in. I wanted to create a short, easy and simple book to read.

One that has steps that anyone can follow on a daily basis should they wish to really impact and change their life but if anything, hopefully it has opened up a new way of thinking for you.

This book is about finding your own truth and what works for you. Take from it what you want and leave what you don't.

Reading this book alone will help you and open your mind.

Remember, you can never go wrong, and even when you think you have, you can always choose again. There are never any doors closed to you. Only new and better ones awaiting you.

The Universe always has your back and is endlessly waiting for you to choose again.

You are all that is, ever was and ever will be. God, source, love, divine energy. We are all one. Individual ripples of a giant ocean.

Be good to yourself as you would to someone you love. Judge not another, for in doing so you judge yourself.

Remember I bring you nothing but angels to help you experience every aspect of yourself. So, you can create the highest version of yourself. Be kind. BE LOVE. Remember who you are.

You are all that is, was and ever will be experiencing yourself through yourself by bringing about situations every day that give you the opportunity to feel and see who you really are.

You are the miracle, you have the power to do all things possible that begins with the choices you make on how you react to everything around you. By understanding your feelings, it gives you guidance to your highest self.

To you my friend, I love with all my heart, I wish you the best experience in this lifetime and every other to come. That you come to know yourself as who you really are.

Time to wake up! That time is now…

ACKNOWLEDGEMENTS

I would like to thank my amazing mum and dad, my four brothers and sister, my whole family and friends who have always showed me both sides to the story of life and who have all helped me to become who I am today.

My husband and best friend Dan, who has been my constant support. My two children Amelie and Noah who are a blessing.

I give my thanks to EVERY single person whom I have ever known, for you have helped shape me and to experience life in every way. For ALL experiences, perceived good or bad have helped me to learn who I do or don't want to be.

"I bring you nothing but Angels", is my favourite saying and everyone I have ever had contact with has been exactly that. Angels or Angels-in-Disguise. A chance for me to know who I am. To grow and learn from you all in this magical experience called life.

A Message from Irene

Thank you for taking the time to read this book and commit to making change for yourself. Hopefully it will have given you a different perspective on how you can make your life one that you love.

I have kept this book intentionally short so that it can be used as a referral for people to revisit time and again. I already have a second book in the making with so much more information to share with you. If however, you feel you want more, then there are a couple of options you can take. You can jump on my online course which will give you a step-by-step guide to lasting change or if you want more personal help, you can work one-to-one with me where we can look directly at what you want help with. I can hold your hand to help you gain clarity and create a plan of action to lead you to the next step forward.

More information can be found on my website
www.ireneremelie.com
Facebook: bit.ly/IreneRemelie

Sending you much love x

ABOUT THE AUTHOR

Irene Remelie, aged 40 lives in the beautiful countryside of
Cheshire with her husband Dan and 2 children,
Amelie and Noah.

She was the youngest of 6 children brought up on a
council estate in a small village. She had a great childhood
with plenty of love surrounding her.
She did not come from a place of money and worked from
the age of 10 on a milk round before school. On leaving
high school, she had a burning desire to enter the world of
entertainment and trained at the Grange Drama School
which led to acting, singing and theatre work.
Irene then travelled the world and on return qualified as a
holistic therapist.

After a near death experience, Irene encountered very
strange and magical events which led her to experience life
on a whole new level. She learned to create a life by
utilising the Laws of the Universe.

Over the years Irene has had a variety of jobs from hotel
management to radio presenting and public speaking.
A qualified holistic therapist, life and business coach and
personal mentor, her aim is to help people make the most
of life and enjoy every experience.

Printed in Great Britain
by Amazon

40126286R10077